LETTERS TO HIM

HONORING FATHERS, GRANDFATHERS, AND FATHER FIGURES

J.J. MATHIEU | DOROTHE PHILIPPE
SYLVIA BECKER-HILL | DANICA RIVERA
STEPHANIE DAUBLE

Along With 14 Inspiring Authors

TABLE OF CONTENTS

INTRODUCTION 5

What's in a Surname?
By J.J. Mathieu 7

The Gentle Way
By Dorothe Philippe 13

Forgiving My Father, Finding Myself
By Sylvia Becker-Hill 21

The Man Who Chose Me
By Danica Alison Rivera 32

With Love, The Girls
By The Dauble Sisters 38

Letter to a Father from a Daughter
By Priya Tandon 45

Breaking Generational Curses: My Father's Legacy
By Rhonda Velez 53

The Unspoken Gifts of a Father's Love
By Alicia Fuentes 61

Honoring The Heroes in My Life: Life Lessons from My Dad and
Grandpas
By Shraddha Chandwadkar 68

Father's Love Comes in Many Forms
By Kelley Rheault 76

Legacy in Action: Lessons Learned and Living One Percent Better
Each Day
By Terri L Trapp 84

The Man Who Gave Me Wings: A Daughter's Tribute to a Legacy of Courage, Grace, and Grounded Strength
  By Helene Su...92

My Father, My Hero!
  By Janet Hamilton 99

Takes Someone Special To Be A Daddy!
  By Anna Barboza Lugo...106

Because I Never Say It
  By Rena McDonald.. 111

Your Life Was Your Message
  By Maria Magdalena Heinrich 117

All That You Are to Me, Dad
  By Johanna Magdalena Posi.. 126

Because of You, I Am HER
  By Wendy Raven Johnson.. 133

Not Too Bad for a Little Mexican from La Grulla:
My Father's Legacy of Faith, Family, Love, and Hard Work
  By Evelina Solís.. 145

INTRODUCTION

There are men whose love isn't always loud, but whose presence echoes through our lives in the most powerful ways. Fathers, grandfathers, stepfathers, uncles, mentors—these are the men who show up, who provide, protect, guide, and love with quiet strength and unwavering dedication.

Letters To Him was born from a desire to honor those men—to give voice to the gratitude, admiration, and love that often goes unspoken. Within these pages are personal letters and reflections from daughters, wives, and loved ones, each one a tribute to the man who made a lasting impact.

This book is more than just a collection of words—it is a legacy. A timeless reminder of what it means to be a father figure and how deeply those roles shape the people we become. Whether the words come from laughter shared, lessons learned, or tears shed, every letter is a testament to the power of love and the enduring influence of a father's heart.

We hope these letters inspire you to reflect, to remember, and perhaps to write your own. Because while time moves forward, the love we carry for these remarkable men deserves to be remembered—and celebrated—forever.

With love and gratitude,
The Contributors of **Letters To Him**

J.J. Mathieu

Author & Astrologer

https://www.facebook.com/jjmathieuauthor
https://www.instagram.com/j.j.mathieu/

J.J. Mathieu is a writer, astrologer and full-time mom with a background in corporate and academic Communication. She earned a Master's Degree in Communication Studies from the University of Rhode Island and is a graduate of Debra Silverman's School of Applied Astrology. J.J. has been writing in a variety of contexts since she was a child crafting fiction books with pencil and spiral-bound notebook in hand. She has worn many hats during her career, but all have centered around or have been influenced by her love of writing. J.J.'s work has appeared on The Barre Blog and MomsIntoFitness.com. Her personal challenges serve as the foundation of her writing, which focuses on inspiring others to see their own lives through a lens of deep compassion and love for themselves and others. In addition to writing, J.J. loves reading, baking, mindful movement and anything chocolate and sparkly. Connect with J.J. at jjmathieuauthor@gmail.com.

What's in a Surname?

By J.J. Mathieu

If I had been born a bouncing baby boy, I would have been named George G. Mathieu, III. No ifs, ands or buts about it, the legacy of the Mathieu surname would have been carried on beyond just the Junior that sits at the end of my own father's name and title. When my mother gave birth to another daughter nineteen months after I was born, the lineage was officially put to rest. To say that the presumed extinction of our family's surname has bothered me for the better part of my life is an understatement. The fact that George G. Mathieu the third, fourth, or even fifth never came to be has been lingering at the back of my overactive mind for a very long time.

It's been twenty years since that beautiful Saturday before Father's Day when my dad walked me down the sandy aisle at Beavertail State Park in Jamestown, Rhode Island. He held my hand with his familiar grip as I maneuvered the borrowed white petticoat and yards of crystal-embellished fabric from my wedding dress down the steps of the trolley that escorted us to the ceremony site. Right before he "gave me away," I remember descending from the final step of the trolley and onto the earth below, sand filling the upper part of my open-toed white silk sandals. "Ugh," I thought to myself. "Not my new bridal shoes." I must have made some sort of outward sound of disgust at the thought of my now not-so-white sandals when my dad interlaced his fingers through mine and asked if I was ready. I smiled up at him and said, "This is it. As ready as I'll ever be." Forgetting my soiled shoes, I allowed my dad to lead me down nature's aisle. I made my way past our guests, who were seated in wedding white folding chairs under the giant white tent that had been erected by the ocean. Distracted by the angst about my dirty shoes and the fact that all eyes were now on me, I forgot to give my dad the traditional kiss goodbye. And to this day, I still regret overlooking such an important detail.

Later on that evening, during the father-and-daughter dance, I got a chance to redeem myself from the forgotten kiss on the cheek as my father and I talked softly while swaying around to the music. We chatted about the ceremony and the reception and how, after years of planning, everything had gone off without a hitch. Before the song ended and we parted ways, my father gave me the best marriage advice anyone has ever shared with me. He said, "Just be happy." I reflected on his words for a moment, realizing that not only were these wise words advice for a happy marriage, but they were also lessons for a happy life and a mantra that he had been living by since he was a young boy, turned doting and loving father.

Shortly after I returned from my honeymoon, I began the process of changing my name. I thought long and hard about my options: keep my name as-is, hyphenate my maiden name with my new married name or go the traditional route and change my maiden name to my married name. I opted for none of the above and decided to make my maiden name a second middle name. Praying that this wouldn't cause too much trouble or confusion with any of the governing bodies that managed name changes, I filled out my paperwork with my new legal name: Jennifer Lynne Mathieu Henshall. Two middle names honoring my past and my future. I was relieved when all of the paperwork was easily processed, and I now had a name that I thought still represented my given surname at birth. I felt a bit of the Mathieu lineage guilt that I'd been carrying with me lift away as I went about my life with a slightly new and unique persona.

Even though my father was blessed with daughters in lieu of sons, he effortlessly (or at least it seemed that way to me) embraced fatherhood and worked hard to give my mother, sister and me a beautiful life. I felt as if I never wanted for anything (okay, maybe my teenage self did feel that way once or twice) and lived very comfortably while under his care until I moved away from home after I graduated from college. Not only did my father do his best to instill the value of hard work and the benefits that go along with tackling and completing the daily grind in me, but he also took the time to play as hard as he worked. I may not have been the most talented basketball player on the court, but he never hesitated to coach me in the driveway and happily attended all of my games. I could always count on him for answers to questions about my math, history or science homework, and he never batted an eye when I needed a shoulder to cry on or a wise ear to hear me out.

One of the things that I love the most about my father is his innate ability to connect with others. Since I was a small child, I recognized his love of connecting with others through nicknames. Once my dad got to know someone, he would grace that person with some sort of funny or apropos moniker. I've been the recipient of a few of them in my day – some I love and some I'd rather forget (i.e., Digger Bob – remember that one, Dad?). However, the nickname that I'm fondest of and still answer to until this very day is J.J. I always assumed that my dad called me J.J. because he secretly wanted me to be named Jennifer Jeanine. Jeanine is my mother's first name, so it made sense that he would want to give his firstborn daughter his wife's first name as a middle name. For 46-ish years, I've walked this Earth thinking that my treasured nickname was a tribute of sorts to my mother and the fact that my father wanted my full name to reflect his beloved wife's first name. However, it wasn't until I began brainstorming ideas for this very chapter, I learned from my mother that the nickname didn't come about in such a meaningful way. In fact, it actually came to be because whenever my baby sister, Christine, tried to say my first name, it sounded more like "Juh, Juh" than Jennifer. But until my dad says otherwise, I'm sticking with the more lofty interpretation of my cherished nickname.

The thing that troubles me most in this world is disappointing my parents – especially my dad. I may be a middle-aged mother of two teenage daughters, but there's still this little girl inside of me who really despises disappointing her father. It's been many, many years since I actually did anything to feel as if I were a disappointment to him. But there are times, even now, well into my adult life, that I feel as if I'm not quite living up to his expectations, which I've learned are really just the expectations I have of myself that have been projected onto him. Honestly, except for those few times in the late 1990s and early 2000s (i.e., in my late-teens and early 20s) when I was testing my boundaries and really screwed up, I feel as if I've been a model daughter. Thankfully, my dad recently justified these feelings to my own 15-year-old by admitting that I was a well-behaved teenager who rarely gave him any trouble. Barring my move to Virginia – 400 miles away from him and my mother in Rhode Island – in 2015, I am fairly confident admitting that I'm still his "favorite oldest daughter."

Ten years and 400 miles later, I still feel extremely close to my father. We have gone weeks without talking, only to pick up our cell phones or log onto our Alexa devices and fall right back into our father-daughter groove. I know that whenever I call my dad to chat, he'll inevitably ask me what's new or how his favorite granddaughters are doing. And he genuinely wants to know what's been happening in our lives. Always one to put his family over himself, during some of the very darkest times in my life, I knew that I could count on my dad for his love and support – no questions asked. He may have once come looking for me in the wee hours of the morning when I was a teenager, late for her curfew, but didn't hesitate to drive me straight through the night back home to Virginia when my family needed me most.

This year, I made a commitment to myself that I was going to take the necessary steps to make my published author dreams come true. My parents – especially my dad – have encouraged my love of writing since I was a young girl, crafting stories with pen and spiral notebook in hand. Since I got married, I've always been of the mindset that I would use my legal name – Jennifer Lynne Mathieu Henshall – on all of my published works. However, since becoming an Astrologer, truly embracing my spiritual side and taking a deep dive into my own soul's promise, I realized that my legal name doesn't quite describe who I am, who I've always been and who I want to be. After a recent Sunday morning phone call with my dad, I discovered that my pen name – a name that not only represents my past, but also my future – had been sitting right in front of me all along. It didn't take but a minute for me to reappoint my author persona to J.J. Mathieu. J.J. to acknowledge not only my mother, Jeanine, but also my sister, Christine. And, Mathieu, of course, to honor my father and his legacy. The first time I officially used my new pen name, it felt like the most natural thing in the world. I may not be George G. Mathieu, III, but I am J.J. Mathieu – author, astrologer, daughter and family surname safeguard. It's my intention for the Mathieu legacy to still live on in the words that I write and on the covers of the books that I put out into the world. Thank you, Dad, for giving me the strength, support and confidence to share my true self – name and all – for all the world to see. May J.J. Mathieu serve as an explicit and everlasting dedication to the unwavering gratitude and love that I have for you now and always. Oh, and by the way, I still owe you that forgotten kiss on the cheek.

Dorothe Philippe

Life coach and mentor in intuition and telepathy

https://www.linkedin.com/in/dorothephilippe/
https://facebook.com/dorothe.philippe?locale=fr_FR
https://instagram.com/dorothe.philippe/?hl=fr
https://www.dorothephilippe.com/

Dorothe Philippe is a life coach, healer and mentor in intuition and telepathy with more than twenty years of experience. She is German living in France and a mother to four grown up children. She has co-authored several books.

The Gentle Way

By Dorothe Philippe

I did not know what to think of you when we first met. I had come to the holiday resort in Greece to take some sun and energy, do sports and recover from the shock of my mom's first cancer operation. We met at the table for dinner. There were six of us. You and your friend Jean-Pierre from France, two young men from the Netherlands and my friend Christine and I from Germany. You were telling a lot of jokes and told me that you had a girlfriend in France, and that she was very pretty. There were a lot of sports activities at the resort, and while I was doing aerobics, sailing and water skiing for beginners, you were on the tatami and with the advanced water skiers. And while I was listening to classical music at 6 p.m. on the beach, you disturbed the peace by doing jumps with your mono-ski. At the end of our stay, the six of us exchanged our addresses and telephone numbers. That was all. A year later, you made a stop at Munich, where my friend and I lived. You were on your way to Austria and asked if we were free for dinner. I was busy with my horse, so you met with my friend Christine. Some months later, you called again. You had come to Garmisch-Partenkirchen, which is about an hour drive from Munich, to participate in a shooting contest between French army reservists and American militaries based in Germany. There was a ball in the evening, and you asked if I would like to be your lady at the table. I was not available again, but we met the following day to go hiking in the mountains. I took you on my favorite walk through the Partnach Gorge, a steep, narrow, beautiful, romantic wild water canyon. You were supposed to leave for Paris, but we decided to take advantage of the wonderful weather and continued the trail up to the top of the mountain to enjoy the view. Time flew by. It was the first time we were alone and without others, and when we found out that we actually had quite a lot in common.

This was the beginning of our love story. One and a half years later, I became your wife and moved to France. We had four wonderful children, stood strong together in difficult moments and never stopped loving and honoring each other until the day you suddenly passed away.

I feel blessed and grateful. You were a loving father and husband, and although I hated jokes, you managed to make me laugh every night before we fell asleep. You never tried to change or to chain me. When I took off to the stables and said I would be back at noon, you laughed and said, "See you tonight then", knowing I would be late. When I came home, you were often waiting for me outside to help me carry the shopping inside. You never disappointed me. You never betrayed me. We were different and still alike. You were my soulmate. I am thankful that we could meet and that we had those wonderful years. I am happy to have told you "I love you" when you were still there, "thank you for all you do for us", and "thank you for being who you are". You have been our hero. You have always been our rock. You have been a helping hand to everyone. I hope that you parted with a feeling of fulfillment and achievement, and that not having become a doctor and not having served in the Foreign Legion were the only regrets you had for your life. You once told me that it was your dream to serve humanity in some way or another. I believe you did. Contributing to peace, calm, harmony, justice, well-being and growth was part of you. You embodied the values you stood by and lived for. You have always been faithful and loyal towards yourself and "the gentle way".

Your mother told me that as a boy, you had a hot temper and easily went off into fights. One day, you hurt another boy seriously. Instead of sanctioning or dismissing you, your school director advised your parents to have you practice judo. Judo then forged your life. It became your way of being. In our bedroom hang the eight core values of judo. The code of judo inspired your whole life and everything you did. Together with the love you had for us and life in general, it became the expression of your soul.

礼 (Rei)
Courtesy
Be polite to others

勇気 (*Yūki*)
Courage
Face challenges and adversity with bravery. Never give up

正直 (*Shōjiki*)
Honesty
Speak and act truthfully

名誉 (*Meiyo*)
Honour
Do what is right and stand by your principles

謙虚 (*Kenkyō*)
Modesty
Be without ego. Keep learning

尊敬 (*Sonkei*)
Respect
Value and respect others

自制 (*Jisei*)
Self Control
Be in control of your emotions, actions and thoughts

友情 (*Yūjō*)
Friendship
Be a good companion and leader

Judo was founded in 1882 by Jigoro Kano, a Japanese educator and martial artist. Kano studied various traditional Japanese Jiu-Jitsu styles, but wanted to create something safer, more systematic and suitable for physical and moral education. Judo was born by observing nature. One day, Jigoro Kano was looking out the window at a snowstorm. He watched as the snow fell on the thick and strong branches of an old oak tree. The snow accumulated, and the oak was able to withstand the weight of the snow. At a specific moment, a branch broke. At that instant, the snow fell on the thin and weak branches of the willow tree. It yielded to the weight of the snow, letting it fall. This observation created one of the basic principles of Judo: "give in to win". Pay attention to the forces. Use your "flexibility" and intelligence. "To the positive, you must oppose its complement: the negative. To force, you must react with flexibility. To the force of the push, give way quickly with a sudden and unexpected recoil. If, on the contrary, an adversary pulls you towards him, pounce in the direction of his traction and then take advantage of his imbalance to knock him down without much effort."

The word "Judo" (柔道) means "the gentle way" from Ju (柔), gentle, flexible, and Do (道), the way or path. Kano considered martial arts as a tool for creating better individuals and, by extension, a better society. This is why he built judo on two main principles:

- Seiryoku-Zenyo, which means maximum efficiency, minimum effort, and
- Jita-Kyoei, which means mutual welfare and benefit.

Kano believed that education through judo should go beyond the dojo. His view was simple yet profound: "Judo is the way to the most effective use of both physical and spiritual strength. By training, one learns to respect others and improve oneself, thus contributing to the prosperity of society."

Judokas bow to one another. Mutual respect creates better relationships and reduces conflict. In judo, there's no room for dominance or hatred. The philosophy of mutual welfare and benefit teaches that your growth should not come at the cost of others. This mindset helps shape a culture of peaceful conflict resolution, a culture of empathy in disagreement and cooperation in diversity. Judo teaches equality and inclusion. On the mat, everyone is equal. Neither your background, nor your job title, your wealth, your culture, your religion or your appearance matters. What matters is your effort, your attitude and your respect for others. Children who grow up in judo learn to respect all people equally, to accept differences and value others for their character, not status. Prejudice fades through shared experience, effort and respect. Judo creates a sense of community. Judo dojos function like small families. They are places where people come together across generations, genders, and cultures to train, support and grow. These micro-communities foster mentorship, encourage accountability and help everybody find belonging and purpose. Judo teaches responsibility and contribution. Higher-ranking judoka are expected to help the lower ranks learn. It's not about superiority, but about serving others with your experience. Kano emphasized this as a civic duty. In this way, judo creates citizens, not just athletes. Personal growth is at the heart of judo. It is not just about learning how to throw or win matches, it is about building character, resilience and life skills. Judo demands mental discipline and emotional control. It requires calmness under pressure. You learn to manage fear, frustration and stress during sparring and competition. Regular training builds emotional and physical resilience. Judo teaches you to lose with dignity and win with humility. No matter how often you fail, you do not give up. You get up to reflect on how you can learn from mistakes and from others. You work on your mindset. You improve your strengths and techniques. The ultimate goal is to become even better. Practicing judo creates confidence without arrogance. Mastering techniques and progressing through belts gives a real sense of achievement and self-worth. Judo is about continuous learning. There's always someone better or a new technique to master. Judo reminds you that perfection does not exist and that personal growth is a lifelong path. Judo is about goal-setting and perseverance. Learning the techniques, moving up belt ranks and competing successfully takes years of practice and hard work. This fosters grit, patience and a goal-oriented mindset, qualities that carry over into all aspects of life. Judo is a school of respect and empathy. From bowing on the mat to helping a partner practice, respect is embedded in everything. Training with others teaches you to understand different perspectives, to support and to evolve together. This helps children and young people build social skills and a positive self-identity. Jigoro Kano's vision was that judo should educate the whole person, his mind, body and character. Judo teaches inner strength, calmness, an open hand and a heart rooted in purpose. Practicing judo helps you to be fully present and engaged in what you do. When you change and become better, your whole environment evolves. Every judoka has learned that the individual is never separate from the whole. When one person grows in discipline, respect and empathy, the whole society becomes stronger. In schools, judo reduces bullying by teaching respect and self-control. In prisons, it has been used to help rehabilitate by building discipline and self-worth. In companies, the values of judo improve leadership and teamwork. Real strength is measured not by how many you can overcome, but by how many you can lift.

Life with you was just beautifully simple. Calm. Steady. We were all so happy. Maybe it is because I am still in love, but thinking of you still makes my heart swell and overflow. I am forever touched by your kindness, your generosity, your strength and your greatness, your love for your children and me, for all life in general. Whatever you did, wherever you were, at home with us, at work in the companies you led or the organisations and associations you engaged with, at sports or as a reservist in the army, you made the world around you a different and stronger place. You always were "the gentle way".

One does not have to be an active judo fighter to bear the values of judo in one's heart. Courtesy, courage, honesty, honor, modesty, respect, self-control and friendship are the solid foundation of all teachings and aspects of life. Your life was about being human and giving your best. I bow to you and thank you for that.

May the spirit of judo and yours go into the world. May it help us grow together to be whole.

Sylvia Becker-Hill

Founder of Becker-Hill Inc.

https://www.linkedin.com/in/sylviabeckerhill/
https://www.facebook.com/sylvia.beckerhill/
https://www.instagram.com/sylviabeckerhill/
https://becker-hill.com
https://sylviabecker-hill.com

Sylvia Becker-Hill is a one-of-a-kind trailblazer in personal transformation and one of the matriarchs of the German coaching industry. Since 1997, she has served thousands of leaders worldwide as their executive coach and corporate leadership trainer. In 2002, she became the first German coach to be certified by the International Coach Federation as a Professional Certified Coach, and in 2023, one of the world's first ten Certified Master Neuroplasticians. As the inventor of the Neuro Creativity™ framework, Sylvia blends science with soul to unlock the brain's capacity for deep healing and bold creation. An award-winning women's empowerment mentor, multiple times bestselling author, energetic edutainer, and soulscapes painting artist, she is a true Renaissance woman. Her chapter in Letters To Him is her love letter to the sacredness of even the most struggling fathers. Her beloved "Papa" passed peacefully in his sleep on September 4, 2019, at the age of 86.

Forgiving My Father, Finding Myself

By Sylvia Becker-Hill

Intimate Moments

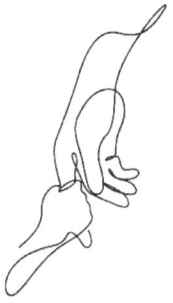

"We search for grand demonstrations of love, yet sometimes it's just a small hand reaching for softness, and a heart knowing it is safe."
~Sylvia Becker-Hill

The four paramedics stormed my parents' house. My father, 86, was in the master bedroom in bed. He had, again, by accident, involuntarily, or out of resistance, not liking it, pulled out his own catheter. The room stank of blood, urine and to his big embarrassment, poop that was on the bed and even on the wall where his hand had left it from his failed attempt to get out of bed. My dad was a very big, very heavy man. Neither my mom nor I were able to get him alone or together, safely out of bed and into the shower; the paramedics did.

Oh, sweet Papa, I will never forget the scared, embarrassed look of your beautiful eyes when you stood naked under the shower, probably with pain and high discomfort, looking into my eyes, pleading without speaking. You didn't have to. **I've always got you.** My whole life, I never understood you intellectually and consciously as I do now, after your death and after learning about trauma, PTSD, and the impact of attachment gone wrong in early childhood. Still, I always got you. I felt you. I loved you.

It was a hyper-stressful situation. Mama freaking out in worry and demented overwhelm. The paramedics were stuck in their rules-filled, limited boxes of work performance. Somehow, there was so much time pressure. Why? I didn't know, but I felt it. Looking back now, six years later, I wish I had had more leadership and told everyone to slow down. I didn't.

But nevertheless, I felt honored by the intimacy of this situation. I, your 52-year-old daughter at the time, showering you, washing you, touching you in places a daughter is not supposed to see, but hygiene demanded it.

When we were finally around 60 minutes later checked in at the urgent care of the nearby hospital, and you wore your hospital gown on your bed with wheels, we talked minimally about the circumstances. I will never forget the one moment where our eyes met again, and deep mutual love and understanding were wordlessly exchanged. **You never were a man of words, but that moment told me everything important.**

A few months later, you left, and it was okay.

Lazy Sunday Afternoons At The Beginning

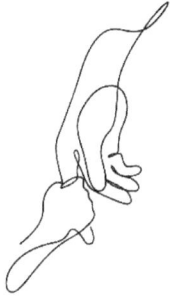

*"We didn't have much—no deep conversations,
no shared creativity—but when I curled into his side and played with his
ears, I had everything."*
~Sylvia Becker-Hill

As a young child, one of my favorite things was snuggling with my dad and playing with—yes, it might sound strange—his earlobes. They were enormous and soft like cotton balls. I must've been a toddler. Yet all I have to do, even now at the age of 58, is close my eyes and touch my own ears, and the memory rushes back. I can feel the velvety texture, hear my delighted giggles. His ears meant comfort. They were magic.

My father was tall, broad-shouldered, with spring-sky-blue eyes. I loved gazing into those eyes, wishing I could dive into them like a mountain lake. I adored him. He was my whole world.

Because of his limited education—cut short by World War II—and both my parents' strong need for safety, he worked in low-paid public servant jobs within the local city administration. For about 15 years during my childhood and teenage years, he had to pay off his brother 50% of the value of their parents' house after we moved in, along with other debts.

Money was tight. So Papa worked two jobs. During the day, he handled city administrative tasks. After an hour of tinkering in his "hobby space" behind the garage—building wooden model ships, fixing machines, or working on the house—we'd eat dinner together, the three of us. Then came the news, one episode of his favorite show, and finally, his night shift as a "night guardian" for the wealthy companies in our town. A mind-numbing, meaningless security job—though one that allowed him to sleep or read if he was only monitoring cameras.

Naturally, **I didn't see him much, and we rarely did anything active together.** When he was home, he was tired. On Sundays, while I went to church with my mother and her parents, he played cards with his buddies at a local pub, came home for lunch, took a nap, and then we'd spend the afternoon watching TV together while my mother worked alone in her beloved garden. She was often frustrated, unable to motivate either of us to join her or help with the large backyard. I imagine she felt left out.

But those Sunday afternoons—snuggled up with Papa watching American TV shows like *The Waltons, Flipper, Bonanza, Little House on the Prairie, I Dream of Jeannie,* and most importantly, *Star Trek,* with my favorite hero Spock—are some of my strongest memories with him. I can still feel the warmth of his big body as I curled up on his left side. That cocoon of coziness, safety, and joy—*us two against the world.*

Judgmental Resenting Feminist

"I rolled my eyes at him for years—until I saw what he survived just to stay gentle."
~Sylvia Becker-Hill

When I became a teenager, our relationship changed dramatically. After years of being a devoted "father-daughter," I shifted and became a staunch "mother-daughter." Suddenly, I felt solidarity with my mother and turned into a rebellious young feminist, judging my father harshly—for his laziness around the house, his refusal to garden, his lack of reading, and his inability to help me with homework. He never engaged in deep conversations, only chatting about the TV shows we both loved. I began to see him as "stupid." I judged him as weak because, when criticized by my mother or her parents, he would shut down, never defending himself. I saw him as socially clumsy—an elephant in a china shop—because he had no filter when guests were around and blurted out whatever crossed his mind about women.

His comments, sadly common in the German chauvinistic *Zeitgeist* of the time, were crass and objectifying:
"Bohhh... look at those boobs! Like a milk bar."
"She's so short, I could rest my beer on her shoulder."
"With those teeth, she makes any horse look like a kitten."

My mother was horrified, often left to smooth over hurt feelings. And I? **I was ashamed.** I felt humiliated to have such a low-class, sexist, idiot of a father.

Later—much later, in my thirties—I began to understand. My father had felt deeply lonely and inadequate. That crude humor, which he'd picked up during wartime camaraderie and his three years in the French Foreign Legion (fleeing his own father's abuse), was a desperate attempt to contribute, to be seen. **He believed, naively, that making other men laugh was his only social currency.** He had no idea what it cost his wife and daughter.

As a teenager, I couldn't see that. I lacked the insight—and the compassion.

I know I hurt him during those "years of judgment," when I desperately wished for a different kind of father: highly educated, intellectually brilliant, socially skilled, charismatic. He was none of that. I don't recall a single meaningful conversation between us besides one strangely magical one about male sexuality, too crude while also too touching to share here, which was impactful and eye-opening for me.

No other man later in my life was as open and vulnerable about men's insecurities around women and sexuality as my father. That a conversation like this might be seen as inappropriate by some people didn't even cross his mind. I always cherished it. I held it as a precious dialogue close to my heart. It felt as if he had opened a door into the male psyche that is normally closed to us women.

The Hungry Boy in a Man's Body

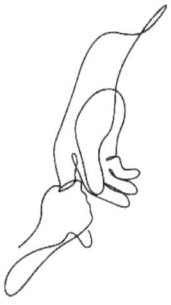

*"I hated his silence until I realized it was built
from screams he let no one hear."*
~Sylvia Becker-Hill

When I moved with my husband and our two young sons—a 3-month-old baby and a 19-month-old toddler—to the U.S., I was thrown without warning into a new world. My husband had received a job offer to relocate from Germany to Michigan just two months before our second son's due date. Suddenly, I found myself in a new climate, immersed in a second language, navigating a culture I thought I knew from Hollywood films and American TV—but I was wrong. They hadn't prepared me for the real United States.

What surprised me most was the constant storytelling, especially during the regular weekend family and neighborhood gatherings in our Rochester Hills suburb, north of Detroit. It was a picture-perfect, white, Christian, middle-class neighborhood with green lawns and picket fences. I had never seen so many child-filled parties, with people trading story after story from high school, college, sports, or about their ancestors—alive or dead.

It was a shock to realize I knew next to nothing about my own family's stories. Almost nothing about my grandparents. Very little of my parents' childhoods or their war experiences. The contrast was painful and a wake-up call!

I flew home to Germany with the boys two to three times a year. Inspired by American storytelling culture, I began asking questions— my parents, uncles, and old neighbors. It wasn't easy. I had to push through inner resistance, breaking an unspoken vow of silence. A cultural taboo. Still, I felt a deep urgency to understand.

Here are a few things I unearthed about my father:

His grandfather was a successful businessman before WWII—tough and authoritarian. He beat my father and favored his older son. My grandmother was cold, order-obsessed, and perfectionistic. I remember how she would inspect our house with a white cotton glove when they came to visit, only to humiliate my mother with a single look, holding up her dirt-smudged finger to her face.

My grandmother locked my father as a boy in the dark cellar for days without food. A neighbor told me she'd slip him bread through the bars. He was also bullied by his brother and classmates. At age 17, to escape his abusive father - who had come home traumatized after years of having been a prisoner of war - he fled on foot to France, joined the French Foreign Legion, and later deserted under gunfire in the Suez Canal, barely escaping alive rather than kill men he considered friends.

My father never hit me. Never raised his voice. **He was a peace-seeking man.** Or rather - I realized - a frightened, frozen in time, unloved boy in an aging body.

No Need for Forgiveness

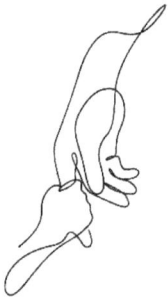

"It's easy to judge what we don't understand—until one day, the story behind the wound breaks your heart wide open and fills it with compassion."
~Sylvia Becker-Hill

All these story fragments—just a few, yet vivid—painted a strong picture of the emotional climate of my father's childhood and youth. Combined with my own professional research as an executive coach since 1997, the latest findings in applied neuroscience and trauma studies, and Germany's long-overdue reckoning with the psychological legacy of WWII—including the epigenetic transmission of PTSD to the war's children and grandchildren—it all finally made sense. **I finally could see why my father became who he was.**

Forgiveness was no longer needed. It dissolved into deep compassion.

Even though my father wasn't an educated man and lived a simple life, he left me with three enduring teachings, passed down not in words but in how he lived:

- Treat everyone—from janitor to CEO—with the same respect.
- Strangers are just friends you haven't met yet.
- Life is beautiful.

Despite the brutality of his early years... despite being bullied by more people than he was loved by... my Pappa never complained.

He remained grateful.

He saw beauty in life.

And now, through my healed eyes and open heart, I see it too.

Danke Papa. Ich liebe Dich.

xoxo,

Sylvia

Danica Alison Rivera

Mom, Joy-Seeker, Counselor, and
Meaning-maker of Life's Scattered Pieces

https://DanicaAlison.com/
https://linktr.ee/DanicaAlison

Danica Alison grew up in the lush landscapes of Oregon, where her love of storytelling and deep connection to family roots began. Now raising two teenagers as a single mom, she brings humor, resilience, and fierce optimism to every chapter of life, including this one. A lifelong nurturer, Danica has opened her heart and home not only to her own children but also to others through foster care, each experience shaping her story in unexpected ways. Starting over in her 40s with courage and curiosity, she is a believer in second chances, late blooms, and the magic of looking back in order to move forward. When she's not writing, counseling, or parenting, you might find her chasing sunsets, dancing in her kitchen, or laughing too loudly with friends. This anthology is her heartfelt tribute to where she comes from and who she's becoming.

The Man Who Chose Me

By Danica Alison Rivera

Dear Dad,

Some fathers are given by birth, and others arrive by choice. You chose me. At ten years old, I became a Rivera, carrying not just a new last name but a new sense of belonging, all because of you!

I still remember the waiting. The build-up to that day felt endless, a mix of excitement and nervous anticipation. I had longed to be a Rivera for as long as I could remember, wanting to share your name, to have it written down as proof of what I already knew in my heart: I was yours. I still remember the day we sat in the courtroom before the judge. You held my hand as we waited for the moment my name to officially change. The judge looked at me, then at my siblings, asking if this was what we wanted. If we wanted you as our father. My heart pounded as I nodded. Before I could even answer out loud, you squeezed my hand, a silent reassurance that the choice was truly mine. It was not just me you were taking on but all three of us. Mom had to love us; she was our mother, but you chose to love us. That choice meant everything to me then, and it still does now. But I did not need to think twice. I wanted to be yours, just as much as you had chosen to be mine. When the judge declared it official, you beamed with pride. You had always treated me as your daughter, but now the world saw it, too.

That day, we went to Izzy's Pizza to celebrate, surrounded by family. I remember feeling something shift. It was not just a legal formality; it was a moment that made me feel claimed, solidified, seen. Becoming a Rivera was not just about a name, it was about belonging. It was about the deep security of knowing I was wanted, that I was not just a responsibility but a choice. You stepped up when you didn't have to, and that truth shaped me in ways I never could have imagined. That moment in the courtroom didn't just give me a new last name; it planted a seed in my heart, one that would later bloom into my own choice to love other people's children through fostering. Just as you had done for me, I would one day choose to love and claim children who needed someone to stand in the gap. Your love became the foundation for how I would show up in the world.

Some of my warmest childhood memories are tied to your presence, woven into moments of simple joys and steady reassurance. You weren't loud or showy in your love, but it was there, in the quiet steadiness of your presence, in the careful patience you showed.

We used to call you Zippy, and even now, the nickname makes me smile. I remember the first time we met you, with your long hair and your laid-back vibe. You did not look like the typical "dad" figure from TV shows, but you were exactly what we needed. You brought your own kind of spark right from the start, full of quirks and energy that made you hard to forget.

You were not perfect, and neither were we, but we all sort of grew up together. You had a way of supporting us in your own way, showing up when it counted, even if life around us was messy. I remember the way you would include us in little projects like building a stool in the garage. It wasn't just about the finished piece; it was the time we spent together, learning, talking, and figuring things out side by side. When you came home from work, your pockets held treasures, gum, candy, little surprises that made the routine of your return feel like an event. On the best nights, we would all pile into the truck for a spontaneous drive-thru ice cream run, because sometimes, life just called for a treat.

You were also the kind of dad who fixed things around the house with a sort of determined creativity, whether or not the tools were right or the parts were all there. And somehow, it worked. I can still picture you duct-taping something together, shrugging and saying,

"It'll hold." And it usually did. You taught us that resourcefulness was not about having it all—it was about making the most of what we had.

And even as I grew older and more independent—more rebellious, even—you stayed true to who you were. I know I pushed boundaries and wanted to do things my own way. There were times I didn't make it easy to stay connected, but you never stopped trying. You did not lecture or chase; you just stayed present. You were consistent, and that mattered more than I ever said out loud. I knew you were still there, still showing up, still willing to be part of my world, no matter how far I tried to run.

I remember you teaching me how to drive. I can still see you in the passenger seat, calm as ever, giving directions, encouraging me, and trusting me even when I did not fully trust myself. And now, years later, you are doing the same thing with my teens. Watching you step into that role again, with the same patience and steadiness, fills me with so much gratitude. You did not stop at raising us; you have stayed connected to all of us. You check in, you show up, and you remain someone we can count on. Whether it is a text, a visit, or a simple moment shared, you have never let the miles or the years create distance.

Even during the rough seasons, when communication between all of us siblings drifted or life pulled us in different directions, you've somehow managed to keep the strings tied. You remind us of each other, of where we came from, and of the love that still binds us together. You never forced connection, but you have nurtured it in quiet ways—family texts, remembering birthdays, making sure no one feels forgotten.

You are a patient man, and you took your role as a teacher in my life into every part of it. You never rushed the learning process but instead guided me with steady encouragement. Whether it was helping me with homework, explaining a difficult concept, or simply engaging me in thoughtful discussions, you made sure I understood rather than just memorized. Your patience made learning feel like an adventure rather than a chore. You loved grading my papers with a red marker, challenging me to go beyond just answering the question and instead think critically. You never accepted mediocrity, always pushing me to do better, to explore ideas deeper, to challenge myself. School was not just about passing for you; it was about learning how to engage with the world in a meaningful way. And through your encouragement, I learned that my thoughts, my words, and my voice mattered.

You also made sure I knew how to throw a ball properly. We spent afternoons playing catch, you teaching me the right stance, the right grip, the right follow-through. You never dismissed my ability because I was a girl. Instead, you taught me with the same patience and enthusiasm you would have taught a son, showing me that strength and skill were not limited by gender. In those moments, with a ball flying back and forth between us, I felt your unwavering belief in me.

One Halloween, I even dressed up as you, complete with your work uniform, learning to read meters just as you did. I cherished being your daughter, and in that costume, I wanted the world to see just how much I looked up to you. It was not just an outfit; it was a tribute to the man who had shaped so much of who I was becoming.

You took us camping, fostering in me a deep love for nature and adventure. Whether it was setting up tents, building campfires, or hiking through the woods, you made the outdoors feel like home. You taught me how to appreciate the stillness of the early morning by the lake, how to respect the land, and how to find joy in the simple things, like roasting marshmallows under a starry sky. Those trips were not just vacations. They were lessons in resilience, in connection, in the beauty of slowing down and being present.

And now, you are the best Papa to your grandkids. As an adult, you have continued to show up in ways that remind me how lucky I am to call you mine. I call you when something breaks, and I do not know how to fix it. You have helped me haul furniture in the back of your truck, assemble impossible-to-pronounce IKEA items, and move into new places more times than I can count. You are still the one I go to when life feels too big or decisions feel too heavy. Your steady advice, your calm presence, and your no-nonsense but kind voice have been the grounding force through many seasons. Even when I did not say it, I always felt safer knowing you were just a phone call away. You stepped into that role with the same love and dedication you had always shown me. You took my daughter to Daddy-Daughter dances, making sure she never felt like she was missing out on the love a father should give. You are teaching my teens how to drive. You have never once wavered in your commitment to being there for the next generation, just as you were always there for me.

You taught me what a father is. And as a single mom, I embrace your lessons and try my best to mirror both mom and dad to my kids. Because of you, I know what showing up looks like. I know what it means to love unconditionally. And I know that being a parent is not just about biology; it is about choice. You did not have to choose me, but you did. And in the way you loved, you taught me what it meant to be family.

To this day, when I think of what it means to be a dad, I think of you, the man who made me a Rivera, the man who made me his.

With all my love,
Danica

The Dauble Sisters

Luxury Reinvention Strategist, Architect of Transformational Storytelling & Founder, The Fullest Stories

https://linkedin.com/in/stephaniedauble
https://facebook.com/sdauble
https://www.instagram.com/daubleganger/
https://medium.com/@stephanie.dauble

Stephanie, Katy, and Terri are sisters shaped by love, shared memories, and the quiet strength of the man who raised them. Stephanie founded The Fullest Stories and Dreamground Collective—a visionary brand strategist and storyteller known for alchemizing insight into soulful strategy. Her work empowers others to rise audaciously into their brilliance. Katy, the heart of the trio, is a licensed massage therapist, spiritual seeker, and soul-led adventurer. Her path has included creative production, caregiving, and healing work across both coasts. Grounded in faith, she leads with presence, intuition, and grace. Terri, the youngest, brings levity, loyalty, and light to every room, with a deep sense of devotion and humor that never fades. A natural connector and trusted confidant, she's also the one who never misses a daily call. Their voices are distinct, but their love is shared. This collection is a tribute to their North Star—the man who shaped them.

With Love, The Girls

By The Dauble Sisters

To My First Home: A Father's Day Letter from Your First Baby, Always By Stephanie Dauble

Before I became anything in this world, I was yours.

You've always been my constant. My compass. My quiet lighthouse in the storm. Long before I knew what the world expected of me—before I learned to be strong, sharp, and soft—you were there: steady, gentle, and full of soul.

It took me years to realize how rare that is—to have a dad who didn't just provide, but who saw me. A dad who showed up at choir concerts, gymnastics meets, and countless tiny milestones—not with fanfare, but with faith. You believed in me before I even had the language to believe in myself. And maybe that's what real love is. Not the kind that shouts. The kind that stays.

I received the gift of watching you raise us and carried the sacred weight of being the first. Your first baby. Your first daughter. Your first co-Santa and the one who made you "Dad." We were both new to it, learning each other in real time. And you—imperfect, devoted, quietly heroic—gave me a kind of love that builds a foundation. The kind that holds steady through storms. The kind that teaches a girl how to come home to herself.

You taught me what it means to be fiercely loyal, quietly brilliant, and unapologetically devoted to faith and family. You taught me that real strength isn't loud—it's patient. It's present. It's the way someone keeps showing up, again and again, even with a bruised heart and trembling hands.

There are moments I'll never forget—quiet shifts in perspective, not sudden revelations. I never needed you to be a hero; I just needed you to be steady. And you were. What I didn't realize then was how much you were carrying—not just us, but your own heartbreak, your faith, your quiet hopes. Now that I've carried some of those same weights, I understand it differently and honor it more deeply.

Your story is stitched into mine and mine into yours—an intricate and complex tapestry of love, loss, and uncommon grace. From before you were ours in the Bonneville pit crew to your years in the classroom, to every time we shared a slice of pie before a long day of Christmas shopping. I see it all. A man who never remarried because he'd already found the love of his life. A father who carried heartbreak with grace. A soul who still sees the world through the eyes of an artist—and still makes his daughters feel like masterpieces.

I'm older now. I've lived. I've lost. I've rebuilt.

But no matter how far I go or who I become, something in me still softens at the sound of your voice. You are the root. The proof. The reason I know what unwavering love feels like.

Dad, everything I am becoming—the poet, the pilgrim, the pathmaker—is possible because of where I began: with you. You were my first safe place. My first audience. My first quiet believer.

Thank you for all of it—for your presence, your patience, your steady hands, and your sacred heart. For the way you've always known me, even in the silences, even when I wasn't sure how to know myself.

I'll carry your love in every chapter of my story.

It's written into my becoming. Etched into my voice.

From your first baby,
Forever and always,
Stephanie

One of One: A Father's Day Letter from Your Little Helper
by Katy Dauble

There's only one.

One man I've measured all others against. One voice that calms me in a way no one else's can. One steady hand I've always known would catch me, no matter how far I fell.

You, Dad. You are my one of one.

From the very beginning, you've been the center of my world. My hero, my protector, my constant. I used to tell people I'd take care of you when you were old—and I meant it. I was three years old when I made that promise, and I've never let it go. I never will.

You've always had a quiet kind of strength. Grace under pressure. Steady in the storm. I've watched you walk through life with a humility that most people don't even understand anymore. You taught me what it means to hold yourself with dignity—without needing applause. You taught me that love isn't about grand gestures. It's about presence. It's about showing up.

And you always did. At every turn.

Some of my favorite memories are the small ones. You calling me your "little helper." Your laughter when we told the "coats" story for the hundredth time. Those silly, sweet moments that stitched our days together. Even now, I still hear your voice in the back of my mind whenever I feel unsure—it's the anchor that keeps me steady.

You've always made me feel safe. Seen. Protected. Whether I was five or forty-five. And more than that, you've never made me feel like I had to be anything other than exactly who I am. That is the rarest kind of love. The kind that lets you breathe. The kind that lets you become.

The truth is, we've walked through a lot together. Joy and grief. Laughter and loss. Big moments and quiet, sacred ones in between.

And through it all, you've never wavered in your love. You've never stopped being the dad I needed—whether I needed a ride, a reality check, or a really good dad joke.

But above all, what bonds us most is faith. You've modeled a kind of faith that isn't performative—it's personal. It's in your character. In your kindness. In your ability to walk through fire without ever letting the flame steal your gentleness. That's what I admire most.

When people ask me about my relationship with you, I say this: We're best friends. We just happen to be father and daughter, too.

I don't know how to thank someone for a lifetime of loyalty, but I'll keep trying. I'll keep showing up for you, just like you did for me. Because I meant what I said when I was little: I'll take care of you when you're old.

You're the only man I've ever known who loved me with that kind of constancy. That kind of patience. That kind of faith.

You are, and always will be, my one of one.

Happy Father's Day, Oak,
All my love,
Katy

Your Everyday Joy: A Father's Day Letter from Your Littlest Girl by Terri Dauble

From family vacations to everyday phone calls, you've always been the heartbeat of my life.

Thank you for everything you've done for me and our family. You've always shown up with grace, humility, and a kind of quiet strength that's rare in this world. Some of my favorite memories are the trips we took—whether they were big family vacations or just our little adventures together. Those moments are etched in my heart, not because of where we went, but because of who I was with you.

I've always felt incredibly lucky that you chose to retire early to raise me. That was no small thing. You didn't just "help out"—you dove into parenthood with your whole heart and humor. What other dad proudly wore the title of "lunch mom"? You did it without flinching—volunteered, no less—and wore it like a badge of honor. That's who you are: Someone who never lets ego get in the way of love. Someone who just shows up.

And you've always been there—whether I noticed it as a kid or deeply appreciated it as I got older. You've been my rock and my safe space. I've been blessed with an incredible support system in our family—Stephanie, Chuck, and Katy—but having you as the foundation of that system made all the difference. You are a great role model. The kind of man who leads not with noise, but with steady presence. The kind of father a daughter can look up to and trust.

I cherish our daily phone calls. That simple rhythm—knowing you're just on the other end of the line—brings more comfort than you probably realize. Whether I'm calling to vent about something or just to chat on my ride home, you never make me feel like I'm interrupting or taking up space. You make room. You always have.

Sometimes, I think about how rare it is to have a dad who is both gentle and strong, who listens as much as he leads, and who teaches not by demanding but by simply living a life of character. You've shaped me in quiet ways, in lasting ways, and I hope you know that, even when I don't say it out loud.

So today, on Father's Day, I want you to know how deeply loved and appreciated you are. Thank you for the memories, the guidance, the jokes, the snacks, the phone calls, the life lessons, and the endless belief in me. Thank you for being my dad—and for being the one I'll always look up to.

With all my love,
Your littlest girl,
Terri

Rudolph Charles Dauble Jr. (Chuck): The Bonus Track

If Chuck were still here, this collection would have a fourth voice—
sharp, hilarious, and impossibly cool in that way only he could pull
off. As the second-born and only son, he was our protector, our
peacekeeper, and the rhythm between sisters. He passed away
unexpectedly on his 44th birthday but remained on life support for
two more days so his organs could be donated—one final act of quiet
heroism. We still feel him in the everyday: a Beatles song, a Detroit-
style pizza no one gets quite right, the sound of a guitar riff in an empty
room, cottage cheese. Chuck didn't need the sun—he was more dive
bar than beach day, more improv than small talk, more soul than
surface. And when "Blackbird" plays, we know it's him. He was, and
always will be, one of us. Our brother. Our anchor. The fourth voice in
this story—and the one who would've just said "Ohh, bohyy."

Priya Tandon

Self-discovery to Personal Reinvention Transformational Coach and Empowerment Mentor

www.facebook.com/thesoulsutras
https://www.instagram.com/priyatandon/

As a Self-Discovery to Personal Reinvention Transformational Coach and Empowerment Mentor, I guide individuals—especially women—through profound life transitions, helping them rediscover their authentic selves and step into their fullest potential. Through a holistic approach blending mindset shifts, emotional healing, and strategic goal-setting, I empower clients to break free from limiting beliefs, build confidence, and create fulfilling lives. Whether navigating heartbreak, divorce, career shifts, or personal growth, my coaching fosters resilience, self-love, and clarity. I integrate proven techniques in emotional intelligence, mindfulness, and personal empowerment to help clients align with their true purpose. My mission is to transform challenges into opportunities for growth, providing the tools and support needed for lasting change. By bridging self-discovery with actionable reinvention strategies, I help individuals heal and thrive, creating a life of confidence, fulfillment, and empowerment. I am also a writer and editor, publishing articles in Coaching Perspectives, Elephant Journal, and Medium.

Letter to a Father from a Daughter

By Priya Tandon

The most important lesson of life you taught me...that everyone should know

Dear Dad,

We have not spoken in over thirty-five years, and it saddens me that I don't know where you are. I wish these words would somehow magically reach your soul.

You are in my cells because, yes, you did give birth to me, but I am part of you—the way I look as I grow older now, the way your nose sits on my face, the way I just murmur something sometimes, or my love for reading and books. Your loving, smiling face never leaves me. I still remember when you would call me Peejee or Piya instead of my given name, Priya- I have not had anyone call me by that name since you left me. I wish I could hear your voice calling for me.

Remember 5:30 p.m.? It was the time you would come back from work. I would stand by the door, and as soon as I saw your silhouette appear at the turn of the road, I would start running towards you with a doll in hand. The neighborhood laughed and knew you were returning when they saw me running. And there you were—just standing there, a little hunched with open arms, waiting to pick me up in your arms for my little hands to reach the sky. I was so happy because you were my sky. I looked at your face—everyone who knew you admired you in different ways—some for your honesty, some for your commitment to work, and others for your love and devotion to your family. Many said you were so handsome, though I did not understand then. For me, you were my dad, and your blue-ish eyes were always generous and kind to me, overflowing with love.

I grew up in your arms, and when I was nearing my fifteenth birthday, you left suddenly, never to return. I remember sitting by the dresser where you kept your watch, which strangely was no longer ticking and was stuck at 10:20 a.m. I remember saying to myself that you would never wear this watch again. I saw your comb sitting on the dresser idly and said, "You will never comb your hair again." I tried combing my hair with it, and it struck me that you were not returning.

I saw the sadness in my mother's eyes and a sudden onslaught of responsibilities in my brothers. My world without you became confusing at that age. I could not cry when I felt your absence, but it started a string of learnings I did not ask for. My world, though, had changed suddenly; the aftereffects of your leaving were gradual and were borne by me in many years to come. I was blindsided and did not see these effects or the learnings coming my way; often, these would creep up from nowhere in the dark of my mind. I became the girl who sometimes wanted to rebel and other times retreat into a shell. I saw my mother and brothers doing the best to hold everything together, but I had abandoned myself with the grief that I didn't even know was grief at the time. I became the strong one—a label attached to me as I grew older and can't be shaken off, unfortunately. Did I say how much I despise being called the strong one? I never communicated with anyone and stored everything—the bad and the ugly—by suppressing whatever I wanted to feel or not feel. It came out in some nameless poor decisions and wrongful acts as a growing teenager in the company of choiceful friends. I did not know this then, but it was only the beginning. This beginning would carry into adult life, leading to arrangements of choices in my life that would first destroy my being before catapulting me into a life worthy of the life you gave me and transitioning into a woman who is finally proud of herself. But I will leave that for another letter—if you get to read this one and reply.

Dad, I learnt many beautiful philosophies and life lessons from you when you were with me. I learnt to be honest in my thoughts, actions, and commitments—responsibilities that could not be shaken off once committed. I learnt to enjoy the simplicity of life amongst books and nature. You always stressed education and "simple living, high thinking" as the mantra. You loved your wife; my mother and I saw you walking with her, especially when she was in an unpleasant mood or something had happened. Although you were not rich, you still managed to make it work somehow. I don't know how you sent your children to private schools on that income! I want to believe you held me in your heart (more than my brothers). You always told my mother that educating me is more important than learning to cook in the kitchen or being someone's wife. Relatives and friends joked that when I married, you would just come with me—that was your attachment to me and mine to yours. I don't think I knew my mother as closely as I do now before you left. Our bond became stronger in your absence. You were never ostentatious or gregarious. Yet everyone knew you and spoke highly of you. I think you were a loyal and simple man until you left. Following your footsteps, I grew up like you—a simple, contented person, devoted to family, unfazed by the materialistic nature of life.

At home, you encouraged me to turn inward and take up spirituality, literature, culture, science, and the history of the world. We discussed how one should lead one's life optimally and worthily to benefit humankind. The teachings were full of wisdom and yet open to debate. Your presence liberated me in my childhood. But where my protected childhood liberated me, my upbringing constrained me in adulthood. Upon reaching adulthood, my upbringing required me to be virtuous and kind to all. However, here was the crisis: in the pursuit of doing the "right thing" for everyone—my ex-partner, family, friends, even a stranger if they asked for my help—my love and kindness for others, in the name of virtue, had turned into a sacrificial ritual. I was like a lamb to be sacrificed before a holy doing. I overlooked the lesson that kindness, love, and giving also have boundaries that should not be crossed. I was just not practical or prepared enough for the world. With the nameless lump of grief following me everywhere, I trusted someone easily whom I should not have. I thought everyone was like you!

But I did learn to be courageous from you.

I had, now, no choice but to be courageous to salvage my thrashed mind, body, and soul, and end everything that I had built and lived for in this lifetime—my marriage, my home, my job. Turns out, I was more afraid of the consequences than of being worthy to all. But in the end, you prevailed by showing me the path to do the right thing for me and embrace my truth. I will spare the details for you since it will pain you to know what I had to endure physically, mentally, and emotionally. I was taken advantage of in what was an abuse of my sovereignty, freedom, and existence. It was not easy, but I chose myself in the end. Somewhere that feeling lingers; if you were with me, you would not have allowed it to happen even for a day. However, this was a lesson in the making for many years, and I had to learn it on my own to become who I am today—a person who enjoys life to the fullest and values every moment given to me to live.

However, the biggest lesson I learned from you—the one that I was still waiting with arms open wide, which I was not ready to accept at almost fifteen when you left, never to return home—is of impermanence. We breathe in and out without paying attention, but I learnt that not even the next breath is promised. There is nothing to hold onto. We may inhale but not exhale, so there is nothing to hold onto in life; the very security that we all crave does not exist. I have understood and embraced it with all my heart. In your absence, the one lesson you did not teach me directly, but that I was left to discover and welcome, is that nothing is permanent. Yet, we must keep living our lives to match our truth of existence with joy and understand our feelings and circumstances. We have to keep moving ahead, we have to let go of what does not serve us, we have to start afresh many times, we sometimes have to break open our hearts to know the meaning of life and what true love means, and still do our best for others with boundaries in place. We have to rejoice in the 'now' with gratitude, we have to forgive for our sakes, because life is beautiful, and what we make of it is in our hands. Impermanence was your gift to me from wherever you are, and I accept it wholeheartedly with love and gratitude. Impermanence showed me a mirror to my soul, echoing that I am my life's creator and hero. I am no longer mad or grieving silently about you leaving me—it does not hurt anymore. I smile when I remember you and always picture you calling me Peejee or Piya with a smiling, handsome face. I am happy and grateful for your few years in my life...and life will keep going on.

My childhood memories are still fresh—they haven't faded with time. I can still smell the evocative scent of earth after a fresh spell of monsoons. With every downpour, the sky waltzed with nature, like the peacock on my front lawn—opening its beautiful feathers to entice the female, unaware of its becoming. This was my abode: an almost flawless, picturesque, and benevolent home at the foothills of the Aravalli range in India. The flamboyant colors of evening are again waiting for me. I am greeting them in the Western Hemisphere, sitting by the fireplace, sipping my hot coffee with the chatter of my children surrounding me. Your absence has taught me that the act of love must be greater than the sum of you and me. This whole equation is created by including you as part of me; there is no other way around it.

We are the embodiment of this heavenly emotion and action of love. We are the unavoidable Love, and we are the whole Universe. Once we breathe in this mantra, we will have no choice but to breathe out the same. We live in a universal society, and we are global citizens. We must omit the boundaries drawn by hate, war, and prejudice to come together and chant this intonation that can unite us all.

I wish you were here with me and your grandchildren. They often ask about you; I fill them in on your stories. I wish I could mail this letter to you at a physical address, but how do I give a letter to someone who has no address on Earth and left a teenager at a fragile age without any warnings? I wish you had not died so soon! So, after almost forty years, this is the best I can do—to write a letter to you and hope you will magically read it. Because that's the other thing you taught me—to believe in blessings and magic.

With love and gratitude
Your now not-so-little darling daughter

Rhonda Velez

Trauma Informed Coach

https://www.linkedin.com/in/rhonda-velez-414a7026/
https://www.facebook.com/rhonda.velez
https://www.instagram.com/realityoflife02/
www.rhondavelez.com

Rhonda is a native California that now resides in Nashville TN, she is a mom, wife, business entrepreneur Driven by empathy and a deep sense of purpose, Rhonda is the Founder of The Tiana Protect, an organization that provides compassionate support to parents navigating the challenging journey of Neo natal or early infant loss. Her unwavering dedication to assisting others through their darkest times is a true testament to her caring nature. As a skilled businesswoman, author and podcast host, Rhonda has been empowering women to achieve success and growth. With her coaching and guidance, women have been able to propel their lives to the next level. She understands that success is more than just financial achievements; it's about finding one's identity and purpose in the process. With a heart full of compassion and a mind focused on empowering others, Rhonda continues to make a positive impact in both her professional and personal endeavors. Her journey is a testament to the power of resilience, love, and the pursuit of purpose.

Breaking Generational Curses:
My Father's Legacy

By Rhonda Velez

When I reflect on the profound impact my father has had on my life, one phrase comes to mind: "breaking generational curses."

My father's story is not just a tale of survival; it is a tale of transformation, of hope rising from the ashes of abandonment and neglect. He was born into a world that could have easily consumed him, a world steeped in pain, emotional scars, and broken promises. His father, ensnared by alcoholism, was never present in his life. His mother, too, was either unable or unwilling to care for him and his siblings, ultimately giving them away to their grandparents. It was a devastating decision, one that left deep marks on my father's soul. While my great-grandparents were good-hearted, loving people, they had already raised their children and had settled into their own lives. Suddenly, they were tasked with raising three more children—children who longed for something more than survival.

Though they did their best, my great-grandparents' ability to give my father and his siblings the emotional support they desperately needed was limited. Survival came first. Providing food, shelter, and protection was the focus, but love and emotional connection, while certainly present, often fell to the wayside. As a child, my father yearned for more—he longed for the embrace of the parents who had given him life but not their presence. He was a child, not yet old enough to understand that the love he craved could not be fully given by his grandparents, no matter how hard they tried.

The void in my father's heart festered. As a young man, he became consumed by anger, resentment, and a deep-rooted desire for acceptance. This pain manifested in rebellious actions, reckless behavior, and a path that led him further into self-destruction. The chains of his past seemed inescapable, as if the generational curses of abandonment, neglect, and despair were destined to define him.

At 17, my father's life took a dramatic turn—an event that would ultimately shape not just his future, but mine as well. On a warm spring night, after a few too many drinks, he and some friends decided to test the limits of their recklessness. They were speeding down a gravel road when my father asked, "How fast can your Chevy go?" The driver, in youthful bravado, replied, "Well, let me show you." Suddenly, the car lost control at high speed, and in an instant, everything changed. The crash was violent. My father was thrown through the windshield, his body hurtling through the air before slamming into the unforgiving ground. His injuries were catastrophic—one side of his face was torn apart, and nearly every bone in his body was shattered. It was a miracle that he survived at all.

Back home, my great-grandfather, a man of unwavering faith, fell to his knees. He didn't just pray for my father's survival; he pleaded with God to spare his life. He begged the Lord to take his life instead, believing that my father had a greater purpose to fulfill, a calling far beyond the tragedy that had shaped his past. As my father lay unconscious, slipping in and out of life, my great-grandfather's faith did not waver. His prayers were relentless.

In the depths of his pain, my father experienced something miraculous. Though unconscious, he felt a warmth wash over him—a sensation starting at the top of his head and moving down to his feet. He knew, at that moment, that something divine was happening. It was as if God Himself was healing him. And in the stillness of his heart, my father made a promise: "God, if You save me, I will serve You."

Two weeks later, despite the devastation his body had endured, my father walked out of that hospital. The doctors were baffled; they had no explanation for his miraculous recovery. But my father did. He knew it was nothing short of divine intervention. From that moment on, his life was never the same. He dedicated himself to serving others, determined to break the chains that had bound his family for generations.

He refused to let his past define him. He left his small hometown of Greeley, Colorado, and set out for California. There, he stepped into a calling far greater than himself. He followed in the footsteps of the one steady male figure in his life—his grandfather—and entered the ministry. His passion? To help the abandoned, the lost, and the broken-hearted—those who, like him, had known the sting of neglect and rejection.

It was during this journey that my father met my mother, Lorraine. They encountered each other while singing in a church choir—a moment my dad would later describe as "the moment I knew she was the one." For my father, it wasn't merely about meeting someone; it was about finding a partner who shared his desire to build the kind of family he had never known, a family grounded in love, faith, and understanding. But as fate would have it, he didn't have the opportunity to speak to her after church that day. A few weeks later, while driving through San Jose, my dad saw my mom pass him in her car. He couldn't believe it. In a spontaneous move, he made a U-turn and followed her. He somehow managed to persuade her to stop, and as he approached her car, he said, "I've seen you before." She laughed and replied, "Sure, I've heard that before." But my dad, never one to give up, recounted the exact moment he had seen her and what she had been wearing. Impressed by his memory, she agreed to go on a date.

Just nine months later, they were married. They were eager to build the kind of family neither of them had experienced growing up—a family rooted in love, faith, and unity. Three years and three months after they said "I do," I was born.

From the moment I entered the world, my father made a conscious decision to be the kind of father he never had. He wasn't perfect, no one is, but he loved deeply, intentionally, and fiercely. I was his "daddy's girl." Whether it was sitting beside him in church, listening to him speak with compassion, or riding with him in the car as he told me stories about his past and the God who had saved him, I always knew he was committed to creating something different for me. I still remember long car rides with him, when we would listen to old Christian music or his beloved Elvis Presley songs.

Though he often worked more than one job to support us—because the ministry doesn't pay well—he always made time for me. One of my fondest memories was spending summers with him at the pizza restaurant where he worked as a technician, fixing the pizza ovens. I'd beg him to take me with him, and when we were done, we'd share a pizza and drink soda out of those red plastic cups. There was something magical about those moments—something about the smell of that pizza place still brings me back to those cherished memories.

As I grew older, I began to see the full extent of my father's impact on others. His dedication to serving people didn't stop at us. He poured his heart into his work, not just talking about redemption but embodying it. He ran a gang center, providing young men a way out of the violent, hopeless lives they had been living. Later, he directed a drug and alcohol rehabilitation program called Teen Challenge, helping people rebuild their lives from the wreckage of addiction.

At the time, I didn't fully grasp the gravity of what my father was doing. It just seemed like something he did, part of the life he had chosen. But as I grew older, I saw it for what it truly was— restoration. My father wasn't just running programs; he was restoring dignity to those who had been broken. He was offering second chances to those who felt they had none. He was showing them that their past didn't have to dictate their future.

I now realize that my own passion for helping others and for changing the next generation was rooted in the way my dad lived. He made mistakes, of course. We've had conversations about his shortcomings as a parent. There were times when his own wounds from the past—his abandonment issues—led him to work long hours, often making him unavailable when we needed him the most. But we've talked about it. I've heard him express his regrets, and I've seen him sincerely apologize for his mistakes.

In that open space of communication, I learned valuable lessons about grace, forgiveness, and self-awareness. I was able to take those lessons and apply them in my own home, with my own children. I learned how to repair things that needed fixing, how to acknowledge my mistakes, and how to be the kind of parent I wanted to be, not just the kind I had known growing up.

My father's life is a living testament to the power of redemption. He took what could have been a tragic, repetitive cycle of abandonment and brokenness, and through faith, love, and purpose, he rewrote it. He broke the generational curses that had haunted his family for years. And in doing so, he gave me a new legacy, a legacy I carry with me every day.

His story serves as a powerful reminder: We are not bound by the wounds of our past. Through God's grace, we have the power to rewrite our stories. We can break the chains of the past and step into the future we were always meant to have.

And that's exactly what my father did.

We all carry stories—some we've chosen, and some that were chosen for us. The truth is, our past has a way of weaving itself into our present, often without us even realizing it. But we don't have to stay stuck in old narratives. With God, healing is possible. Redemption is possible. A new story is possible.

As you sit with your memories and moments, I want to invite you to reflect honestly and tenderly on your journey. Consider these questions—not as a checklist, but as an invitation to explore, to heal, and maybe even to begin writing a new chapter:

- What stories from your past have shaped how you see yourself, your relationships, and your purpose?
- Are there patterns in your family history—spoken or unspoken—that you've carried with you into adulthood?
- In what ways have you allowed your past to define your worth, your choices, or your future?
- Have you ever considered which parts of your story God might want to redeem?
- What would it look like to invite God into your healing process and ask Him to help you rewrite the parts of your story that still hurt?
- What generational patterns are you being called to break, or your freedom and for the legacy you're leaving behind?
- Where is God inviting you to step into something new, even if it means leaving behind what feels familiar?
- How can you offer grace to the generations before you, even as you choose a different path moving forward?

Alicia Fuentes

Founder and Certified Coach

https://www.linkedin.com/in/alicia-fuentes-feminineleader/
https://www.facebook.com/aliciazfuentes
https://www.instagram.com/alicia.feminineleader
mypowerunlocked.com

Alicia Fuentes is a Feminine Leadership Coach who works with women in leadership, who are ready to embrace their feminine energy, step into their full power, and lead with confidence and ease. She helps them embody a powerful presence, embrace freedom and flow, and elevate their influence and impact, thereby transforming their journey into one of empowerment and purpose. Alicia believes that feminine leadership is a powerful force—one that thrives not by mimicking traditional masculine models but by embracing intuition, flow, and authentic power. True leadership isn't about pushing harder or proving yourself; it's about leading with confidence, ease, and a deep connection to your unique strengths. She has successfully guided women through transformative processes, helping them shed outdated beliefs, trust their feminine energy, and embody a leadership style that feels natural, effortless, and deeply impactful. Her method transforms high-achieving women from feeling stuck and uncertain into trailblazing leaders who own their presence, make aligned decisions, and create lasting influence—without sacrificing their well-being or authenticity. She is a certified coach, published author and speaker with expertise in empowering women through their leadership journey, incorporating Neurolinguistic programming and timeline therapy, where needed. Alicia holds a BSc. and MPhil. in Chemistry, is a Chartered Health and Safety Professional and is certified in coaching through She's in Business's Dr. Stephanie Wilson and Tony Kaye's ProCoach programme. Outside of coaching, Alicia loves playing with her fur baby Zoey, spending quality time with her family, meditating and writing, which help her stay balanced and energized.

The Unspoken Gifts of a Father's Love

By Alicia Fuentes

It's in life's quiet moments that we truly begin to understand the depth of a father's influence—not in grand gestures, but in the steady way he quietly holds the world together. My dad's life is a testament to resilience, love, and unwavering dedication. His journey has been one of quiet heroism, marked by the values he lives by and the legacy he continues to build.

My dad is a true problem solver. He believes that every problem has a solution, and he approaches challenges with a creative and positive mindset. Whether it's a business challenge, a family dilemma, or something practical around the house, he rolls up his sleeves and figures it out. He taught me that even if a solution isn't obvious at first, if you stay curious and calm, you'll eventually find your way.

Some of my favorite times have been watching TV with him late at night, when conversations would flow naturally into stories from his childhood. As the eldest of six, he always had a story—mischievous tales filled with adventure and laughter. Even as an adult, he was often the one bailing out siblings from tricky situations. He would light up when there was a good Western on, such as *Abyss of Passion*, or when I bought him a Louis L'Amour Western novel. Those stories transported him, and I could see the joy they brought.

Two vocations I believe are worth highlighting. One has been his service as a Rotarian (1998–2014) and his presidency from 2009 to 2010. He took this role seriously, finding joy in helping others, especially those less fortunate. It came naturally to him.

The second has been his enduring devotion to the Catholic Church. Although he taught at a Presbyterian school, he remained steadfast in his faith. Dad served on committees, supported fundraisers, read at Mass, and even offered janitorial services from his company—all done quietly and without any expectation of recognition.

His gift-giving is always thoughtful and intentional. He never buys without meaning—whether it's for birthdays or milestones—he listens, reflects, and chooses what would speak directly to your heart.

Though I wish we had traveled more, our trip to England was unforgettable. I was receiving an award from my organization and brought him along. Walking the streets of London, visiting Buckingham Palace, Big Ben, and pubs—just sharing time as tourists—it was one of my proudest moments. I loved seeing him relax. Even our beach outings give me that same joy. The little girl in me always wants Dad to rest, to unwind, because he works so hard and gives so much to everyone.

One of the most vivid memories of courage and resilience is the 1988 fire. Our home was completely destroyed. Despite the fire station being just a few meters away, they couldn't find our house in time. My dad broke his left arm trying to fight the blaze himself. I never saw him cry, but I know he did—all that he and my mom worked for was gone in minutes. But he never gave up. Within a year, he rebuilt a new, better home for us. That's who he is.

I still remember the pride I felt when he gave me his secondhand Toyota Corolla while I was pursuing my master's degree. It wasn't just a car—it was a gesture of belief in me, in my future.

Dad taught primary school for 40 years. It was his calling. He gave his all to shaping young minds. To this day, his former students—now professionals—never pass him without greeting. They still call him "Sir" with respect and affection.

Just as he shaped young minds in the classroom, he's continued to lead with the same clarity and conviction in the world of business.

Lately, I've been fortunate to witness Dad in his element—as the businessman. For years, I wasn't involved in the family business and didn't fully grasp the depth of his talent. But witnessing him recently, at 75, negotiate contracts, pitch services, and command respect with such passion and poise, filled me with awe. He's sharp, eloquent, and deeply respected. In that moment, I realized how much I still want to learn from him. Watching him reminds me of the kind of leader I hope to be—one who leads with consistency, fairness, and heart.

Yet, in the fullness of this story, I want to be honest. My dad, like any man, is not perfect. He's human. There were times when he struggled to balance the demands of his two careers. His marriage to my mom had its rough patches, and as children, my brother and I didn't always agree with him. But these moments don't take away from who he is. They make him real. They remind us that greatness isn't the absence of flaws but the presence of perseverance, of trying again, of love shown in action.

What always carried him through—and what he's leaned on more and more as he's grown older—is his faith in God. As a Catholic, his spiritual foundation has been strong since we were children, but in his later years, especially after his heart attack and some health struggles, his faith has become his refuge and strength. He believes in God's presence and work in his life without question. That quiet, steady belief has not only sustained him, but it has also shaped me.

Even when I was living abroad, first in Italy, then in Egypt, there were sometimes long stretches where we didn't speak often, and I missed him deeply. Being so far away from him during those years helped me appreciate his presence even more. His quiet wisdom, his voice on the phone, even the messages he would sometimes send—they meant more than I can say.

Now, as I write this, I realize there's so much I don't know about his life. It's a reminder that sometimes we get caught up in our own worlds and forget to ask about theirs. Fathers often carry silent burdens so that their children can feel safe. My father was no different. He stood strong for us—even when he may have been uncertain himself.

Lessons I've Learned From My Father

As I reflect on my father's life and the lessons he has imparted, I realize that his impact is not just in what he did, but in who he is—and in the quiet wisdom he passed down. Here are the core lessons I carry forward, shaped by his example and refined through my own journey.

Perseverance

Dad taught me that setbacks aren't the end. Whether it was rebuilding our home after a devastating fire or managing his business at 75, his perseverance inspires me to keep going, no matter the challenge.

Service

Through his quiet acts of giving to his church, family, and community, Dad shows me the true power of service. He never seeks recognition; he simply gives because it's his way of making the world a little better.

Resourcefulness

Watching him solve problems—big and small—teaches me that creativity often emerges in the face of adversity. Dad shows me that there's always a solution if you approach things with an open mind and resourceful hands.

Steadfastness in Faith

His unwavering trust in God has been a foundation for both of us. In moments of uncertainty, I turn to his example, finding strength in faith as he always has.

Love in Action

Whether it's through thoughtful gifts or simply showing up when needed, Dad expresses love in his actions more than words. His quiet support has shaped my own approach to love through deeds, not just declarations.

Hard Work, but at What Cost?

His hard work brought success, but I've come to see that it also came at a cost—time with family, health, and rest. Now, I strive for balance, embracing my ambition while also prioritizing my well-being.

Kindness over Judgment

Dad's advice to never judge others has stayed with me. Even when I catch myself making assumptions, I remember his calm voice, encouraging me to pause and consider the bigger picture. His wisdom continues to guide me through life's overwhelming moments.

Grace for Human Imperfection

Dad is not perfect, but he never stops trying. He has taught me that imperfection is part of being human, and what matters is showing up, loving, and growing. This lesson has helped me embrace my own flaws and keep moving forward.

My deepest wish for him now is peace. To live the rest of his life knowing that he did his very best—with love, fairness, and an open heart. He can finally rest and do things simply because they bring him joy. May he feel proud of the life he has lived, the children he has raised, and the legacy he will leave behind. I want him to know it's okay to rest now, to enjoy hobbies, to bask in the love he's given so freely.

Reflecting on all the qualities that make my dad such an incredible man, I realize just how much he has shaped me into who I am today. The lessons he has taught me—through both his strengths and humility—continue to guide me. I am proud to be his daughter, and I will carry his example with me, always striving to live with the same kindness, wisdom, and faith that he has shown me throughout his life.

A Note to the Reader

If you are blessed to have a father—or someone who stood in that role—speak to him. Ask him about his life. Listen. Honor his story. If you grew up without a father or father figure, I hope this story offers a glimpse of the love and guidance that such a presence can bring. Know this—fatherhood is not just a biological role. It's about guidance, protection, and love—and sometimes, those come from other places: uncles, teachers, mentors, spiritual leaders, or even friends. Honor those who showed up for you. Let us not wait for time to slip away before we acknowledge their sacrifices, their love, and their humanity.

Because sometimes, the quietest heroes leave the loudest legacies. My dad, Selwyn Fuentes, will be one such hero.

A Letter to My Father

Dear Dad,

If I don't say it enough—thank you. For your strength. For your love. For the quiet, steady way you held up our family, even when it meant putting your own needs last. You've shaped me more than you know.

And now, I hope you allow yourself the peace you deserve. Do the things that bring *you* joy. Read your Western novels, take your time, laugh more, rest deeply. You've done more than enough.

I carry your lessons in my heart. I live by your example. And I hope to lead with the same integrity, compassion, and faith you've shown me all my life.

With Love Always,
Your daughter Lisa

Shraddha Chandwadkar

Self Esteem and Mindfulness Coach

https://www.linkedin.com/in/shraddhachandwadkar/
www.instagram.com/luminouslifelabs
www.shraddhachandwadkar.com
info@shraddhachandwadkar.com

Shraddha Chandwadkar is a passionate Self-Esteem & Mindfulness coach who empowers women and children. Her workshops, coaching sessions & mini retreats focus on practical strategies to improve confidence, self-image, overcome self-doubt, and develop a positive mindset. They also include mindfulness techniques to increase self-awareness. Shraddha is a published author and has coauthored two bestselling anthologies "Becoming an Unstoppable Woman in Health and Wellness Part 2" and "Pray Don't Panic." She is also a Reiki Master and volunteering as an executive program director in a health and wellness non-profit. She received the 'President Volunteer Service Award' in 2024 acknowledging her service. Shraddha is a mother of two teens and three cats and a spiritual seeker who loves to spend quality time in meditative & contemplative practices. An Engineer by education, Shraddha has an MS, Computer Engineering, from NC State University USA and Bachelors in Electronics Engineering from Pune, India.

Honoring The Heroes in My Life: Life Lessons from My Dad and Grandpas

By Shraddha Chandwadkar

As Father's Day gently draws near, it presents a poignant moment to celebrate the remarkable men who have shaped my world. My childhood blossomed under the distinct and loving care of my father, paternal grandfather, and maternal grandfather. Observing their individual paths and the essence of their being in my life has undoubtedly imparted profound wisdom. I share some of the invaluable lessons below.

Resilience and Growth Mindset

My resilience has been forged in the crucible of life's experiences and the tapestry of individuals who have graced my path. Growing up in a modest middle-class home in India, nestled with my parents, younger sister, paternal grandfather, and great-grandmother, my early years held both shadow and light. The specter of my father's alcoholism cast a long shadow until I reached the age of fifteen, painting many nights with tears, sadness, anger and frustration. Yet, this was not the sole tableau of my young life. With profound courage, my father confronted his formidable challenge, daring to seek help and embrace vulnerability. Within a single year of resolute decision and heartfelt prayer, he emerged from the grip of alcoholism, a freedom he cherishes to this day. The unwavering support of my mother and his friends, along with the fellowship of Alcoholics Anonymous, undoubtedly played an indispensable role in this transformation. Moreover, my father's journey did not end with personal triumph; he went on to excel in executive roles, lending his expertise to the flourishing of numerous businesses.

Even while navigating his own significant challenges, he actively fostered my independence and resilience. Encouraging me and my sister to undertake the Garhwal Himalayas trek to Harkidoon in the 7th grade is a powerful example of this. It speaks to his belief in our capabilities, his desire to expose us to challenging and enriching experiences, and his willingness to let me step outside of my comfort zone. That kind of early exposure to adventure and overcoming physical challenges can indeed build significant inner strength.

Similarly, his reaction to my academic setbacks during engineering college was incredibly insightful. Instead of resorting to blame or criticism when I didn't score well, his consistent message of "study hard next time" fostered a growth mindset. This experience helped me view academic challenges as opportunities for learning and improvement, rather than something to fear or feel guilty about. His unwavering support in those moments has been instrumental in building my capacity to face difficulties head-on, without resorting to avoidance or self-recrimination. It is clear that his actions, even in the face of his own struggles, were intentionally geared towards empowering me.

My father is a deeply caring and selfless individual. My experiences with a persistent dry cough during my younger years highlight his quiet devotion. Stepping in to care for me at night when my mother was occupied with my sister demonstrated his consistent and loving attentiveness. His efforts to alleviate my severe dry skin, ensuring I had warm water soaks and applying the precious Nivea, further underscore his commitment to my well-being. The fact that he never complained about the expense speaks volumes about his priorities.

Some of my most cherished moments with my father unfolded while watching the captivating matches of cricket or the elegant championships of Wimbledon. We were utterly enthralled by these sporting events, often losing ourselves in hours of enthusiastic viewing.

My parents understood the importance of inner strength and modeled it through their own experiences, providing me with a powerful foundation for navigating life's complexities. Their focus on resilience over superficiality has undoubtedly shaped my perspective and my ability to cope with adversity.

Frugality and Discipline

My paternal grandfather's story is a powerful testament to selflessness, resilience, and unwavering dedication to his family. His decision to leave his job at the relatively young age of 40 to become the primary caregiver for my father, aunts, and great-grandmother after the early loss of my grandmother speaks volumes about his character and the depth of his commitment.

Despite not being wealthy, his frugality was a strength that enabled him to provide for his family. Living off his savings and yet managing to purchase an apartment and ensure his three children received an education highlights his careful planning and responsible nature. His modest lifestyle, indicated by owning only three or four pairs of clothes and diligently repairing them himself, underscores his resourcefulness and practicality. Even as his eyesight began to weaken, his request for help only with threading the needle, while maintaining his independence in other tasks, reveals a strong sense of self-reliance and a desire to remain capable for as long as possible. His life exemplifies sacrifice and the quiet strength it takes to prioritize family well-being above personal gain.

My paternal grandfather's commitment to his physical well-being and his disciplined lifestyle are truly admirable and offer further insight into his character. He clearly understood the importance of proactive health management. His consistent daily routine, waking up at the same time and adhering to timely lunch and dinner schedules, speaks to a strong sense of self-discipline and order. The fact that he diligently walked 3–4 miles every day well into his 80s, coupled with his consistent home exercise routine, underscores his dedication to staying physically active and maintaining his health as he aged.

Beyond the rich experiences he cultivated, his nightly ritual of immersing himself in books illuminated a deep commitment to lifelong learning and intellectual curiosity. It was through my grandfather's gentle introduction to the vibrant pages of National Geographic, teeming with exotic animals and colorful birds, that my young mind first encountered the captivating beauty of the toucan and painted bunting. His engagement with the written word went far beyond mere reading; I recall him meticulously underlining unfamiliar words and diligently consulting his dictionary, ensuring a thorough understanding. Key insights and significant passages would be thoughtfully highlighted or underlined with his pen, a testament to his active and engaged approach to learning.

His choice of a vegetarian diet and the daily practice of drinking lukewarm water point towards mindful and healthy habits. The remarkable fact that he rarely needed to visit a doctor throughout most of his life is a testament to the effectiveness of his disciplined lifestyle and proactive approach to health. His method of addressing minor illnesses like colds and the flu by simply resting and adjusting diet reflects a natural and perhaps intuitive understanding of his body's needs. This holistic approach to health, prioritizing consistent healthy habits and trusting in his body's ability to recover from minor ailments, instilled a powerful example of self-care and responsible living.

His consistent expectation of me being out of bed by 8:00 a.m. on weekends, a time when many might choose to sleep in, speaks to his emphasis on a form of "tough love" rooted in a desire to instill discipline and perhaps ensure I didn't waste my days. The image of him singing to rouse me from sleep adds a touch of warmth and personality to his firm approach. It wasn't just an order; it was a gentle albeit persistent nudge towards being active. This method likely instilled in me a sense of routine and perhaps appreciation for starting the day early, even on days off. It is a unique and memorable way he showed he cared, not by indulging me with lazy mornings but encouraging me to get up and engage with the day.

Unconditional Love and Purposeful Living

My maternal grandfather was a truly gentle and devoted soul, and my memories with him paint a picture of deep affection and spiritual connection. His piety, love, and care are evident in his actions towards me.

The overnight train journeys from Pune to his home in Hyderabad, Andhra Pradesh (now Telangana), India, during my elementary years have been special experiences, forging a unique bond between him and me. His willingness to undertake these trips with me highlighted his desire to spend time with me and share his life in Hyderabad, India. Despite the challenging summer heat of Hyderabad, which often led to me falling ill with nosebleeds or fever, his loving care shone through. The image of him massaging my feet with a special metal bowl to alleviate my body heat is particularly tender and speaks to traditional remedies and his attentiveness to my comfort.

Furthermore, his practice of reciting stotras and shlokas in the mornings and encouraging me to repeat after him not only introduced me to spiritual traditions but also created intimate moments of learning and connection. This sharing of his faith and values was undoubtedly a significant aspect of my relationship and instilled in me a sense of spirituality and cultural heritage. These memories illustrate a profound bond built on love, care, and sharing of faith in divinity.

He also had a knack for creating memorable experiences and instilling important values in me. The contrast between spooky night-time ghost stories, which he skillfully made believable, and the serene mornings filled with faith, fearlessness, and humility was fascinating. He knew how to engage my imagination and perhaps gently test my courage with his tales, while simultaneously grounding me in faith and positive principles. This balance of playful storytelling and spiritual guidance has been quite impactful in my formative years.

His great love for roses and fish further reveals his nurturing and gentle side. Cultivating 30 rose plants on the terrace of a rental apartment and caring for them like children, resulting in hundreds of blooms, speaks to his patience, dedication, and appreciation for beauty. Similarly, his meticulous care for his fish tank, ensuring the well-being of the fish, demonstrates his kindness towards all living creatures. These passions added another layer to his character, showing a man who found joy and purpose in both the spiritual and the natural world around him.

His hobby of making *attars*, those exquisite natural perfumes, adds another dimension to his rich and multifaceted personality. It speaks to a connection with natural scents and a potential for artistry and craftsmanship. This unique interest surely made him even more distinctive and memorable.

The fact that he was able to visit me in the U.S. at the age of 86, accompanied by my uncle and aunt, is a testament to his vitality and my family's desire to share his presence. Furthermore, his purposeful engagement with crossword and sudoku puzzles right up to the age of 91 highlights his sharp mind and his commitment to staying mentally active. His life of contentment and cheer, coupled with his deep love for all his grandchildren and his consistent engagement with spiritual books, further emphasized his intellectual curiosity and his inner peace. He truly lived a full and meaningful life, leaving behind a legacy of love, learning, and a positive spirit.

It is beautiful how the people who've touched our lives most profoundly aren't always those with the most material wealth.

Instead, they enrich us with something far more valuable: the deep experiences born from their purposeful living, their unwavering hard work, their steadfast discipline, and their remarkable resilience. The gratitude I feel for these heroes, who nourished me with such profound love in their unique ways, speaks volumes about the true riches in life. A BIG THANK YOU from the depths of my heart!

Kelley Rheault

Founder / Owner / Success Coach

https://www.linkedin.com/in/kelley-kaupas-rheault-5705a31a
https://www.facebook.com/kelley.rheault
www.purple-camo.com
https://linktr.ee/PurpleCamo

Kelley is a Florida native from Fort Lauderdale. She joined the Air Force after high school and served for 6 years as an Airborne German Linguist. After her military service she attended Montana State University and received her BA, with a focus on International Business. She became a business owner running her own agency with LegalShield in 1997. In this role she has worked with many large multinational companies, trained hundreds of new agents, spoken in front of numerous groups, received recognition as the #1 associate in the State of Florida and is currently ranked as one of the top 20 associates worldwide. In 2018 she received her life and business coaching certificate and launched "The Transitioning Warrior", a Veteran's organization that supports military men and women in discovering their purpose and passion after they leave the military. Her mission is to empower others to live their best life!

Father's Love Comes in Many Forms

By Kelley Rheault

Days after I was born on 02/04/68, it became very apparent that my mom was not able to care for me, as she was unable to care for my older siblings.

My biological father was out of the picture as of about a month ago. Because of his drinking and abuse, he almost caused my mother to have a miscarriage with me at eight months in utero. That incident was the final straw, and within a couple of days, he was driving west out of Phoenix and heading towards some random city in California.

That was the last time he would ever see me, thus starting my story of growing up never knowing or meeting my biological father.

My older brothers, Derek and David, and my older sister Kimberly were already living with Wanda and Jesus (Chuy). It was the best foster home that my brothers had ever been in, having gone through so much physical and emotional abuse in previous homes.

They really felt like they won the lottery with Chuy. He was a hunter and a fisherman and had this pale-yellow pick-up truck that took them on all their adventures. They said they would never forget that truck!

My sister was only three and a half years old, the youngest foster child they had ever had, and they were already very attached to her. So, when the call came in from Maricopa County asking if they'd be willing to take in a newborn, from this same family, hoping to keep the siblings together, it wasn't as easy a decision as they thought.

They were getting so emotionally attached to my siblings and thinking of having a brand-new baby in the home, they just didn't know if they could handle it emotionally.

I am extremely grateful for their big hearts and that they just couldn't imagine not keeping our little family together... they said yes... and my life was changed forever!

The four of us, along with Wanda's older biological children popping in from time to time, lived a modest yet very caring home life. Chuy was born in Mexico, and our kitchen smelled like tacos, tamales, and fresh homemade tortillas on most days. Even as a toddler, I enjoyed this cuisine and demanded hot sauce on my scrambled eggs.

Chuy worked hard for and retired from the City of Phoenix, and was gone before sunrise on most days, so Wanda stayed home and was our amazing day-to-day caregiver.

Enjoying my days growing up with this wonderful family, I could have never imagined that at around two years old, I would be ripped away from this wonderful man, the only father (papa in Spanish) I had ever known.

My mother, although she was in and out of mental hospitals, was able to come visit us, usually for just a few hours, never sleepovers. So, Wanda and Chuy were very alarmed, and even called their case worker when she asked to take us for the weekend. She asked them to pack bags for the four of us, and when she pulled up in her old car, with the brakes squeaking loudly enough to be heard down the street. Wanda and Chuy were told they had no other choice but to let us go with her.

The weekend was over, and there was no sign of us... Extreme panic was setting in, and they were fearing the worst. After many sleepless nights, a call finally comes in from Fort Lauderdale, Florida, about 2,400 miles away from Phoenix. To say they were shocked was an understatement, and how we all survived this lengthy road trip was a miracle in itself and could be a made-for-TV movie for sure.

During the call, they learned that she only had my sister and me, and the reason for her call was to ask for $500 to sell me to them. Of course, they never considered her offer, but they were so overjoyed to have heard from her and to know that all four of us were safe. My brothers had been dropped off 250 miles north, with my mom's brother.

Wanda and Chuy booked flights immediately and flew to Fort Lauderdale with hopes of bringing us home. Little did they know the situation would turn even more tragic, because my biological maternal grandmother and other family members suddenly wanted to be heroes, fighting to keep us in Florida. Where had they been the last four years?

When Wanda and Chuy arrived in Fort Lauderdale, they were directed to my great aunt's real estate office in Plantation. Little did they know this was probably the last time they would ever see me. I sat on Chuy's lap, so happy to see my papa, and could see tears in his eyes, as he listened to my biological family tell them that they had no rights as our foster family in Florida. They continued telling them they would not be taking us back to the only home that I had ever known, their home in Phoenix.

I later found out that as I sat in my father's lap for the last time, I asked him why he was crying. It was the last conversation we would have, and with tearful hugs and kisses, they left the real estate office. The drive back to the airport was somber. They were completely heartbroken. It was a long, extremely heartbreaking journey back to Phoenix without their children.

I went on to move around with different family members, as my mom was readmitted into the local mental hospital. Eventually, my mom's sister, Rosemary, moved from Phoenix to Fort Lauderdale to step up for her nieces and nephews and help however she could. That help resulted in my aunt becoming the legal guardian of my oldest brother, Derek, and me. She said she wished she could have taken all four of us, but thought the oldest and the youngest were the best option she could afford at the time. Unfortunately, my brother, David, and my sister went on to be in and out of numerous homes. Homes that tragically even included living with my mom, as she continued to struggle with mental illness.

Thankfully, my brother David found his way back to us first, and a couple years later, after another long-term foster home stay that she had to endure, my sister came to live with us. She was around 10 years old, and we were finally reunited and living under the same roof again. We were all so grateful that my aunt stepped up for us another time. She went to the courts and became her legal guardian, too.

So, what was going on with Wanda and Chuy, my first family, back in Phoenix? After they lost us, they were so devastated and heartbroken that they promised each other they would never foster again. But there was a grander plan in the works for them, and soon after they returned to Arizona, one of their tenants, in the mobile home park that they managed, gave birth to a little girl. She was in need of a loving family because her mother was an addict, and she was born with many health issues. Only by the grace of God were they able to fully adopt this little child, this little girl, whom they named after the two foster girls that they loved and lost. In an instant, I had a namesake I knew nothing about, Kelly Jo.

I tell you that part of the story because it's the only reason that in 1989, when I married Patrick, whom I met in the Air Force when we were stationed in Germany, Chuy was the one who walked me down the aisle. How in the world was that possible? How were we ever reunited? I know this is going to sound contrived because it truly is an unbelievable story, but here is how we miraculously were given another chance!

Wanda and Chuy liked taking Kelly camping in the remote Arizona mountains in areas off the beaten path. During one of their trips, there was another family, with a little boy and a girl, camping not far off. And as children do, the three of them became fast friends and played together. This gave the parents a chance to meet. It must've been divinely inspired, but a conversation came up about how the children got their names. Wanda and Chuy proceeded to tell the couple how Kelly was named after the foster girls they were forced to give up. Hesitantly, the mother of the children said, "Wait, was their mother's name Norma, and their aunt named Rosemary?" In complete shock, that almost took their breath away, they said yes... "How could you know that?" And with tears in her eyes, Carol said, "Rosemary is one of my best friends and I'm in contact with her... She still lives in Florida. Would you like her number?"

The most beautiful words they had ever heard... and with her heart beating out of her chest, and still in complete shock, Wanda said, "OH MY GOODNESS, YES, ABSOLUTELY!!!" They could not believe that their prayers had been answered, and by a random family in the middle of the woods, no less. They just might have a chance to see their four beloved foster children again.

Only a few days later, the phone rang in our home in Fort Lauderdale, and I was the one who answered it. When the couple on the other end of the phone described who they were, I was very confused because I had never heard the story of a foster family in Phoenix, and especially this wonderful man, who was the only father I had ever known. The only stories I had ever been told were that my father was a bad guy and an alcoholic, and he never saw me after I was born.

That summer, Wanda and Chuy flew Kim and me out to Phoenix, to a house they had moved to, within walking distance of the one we lived in as small children. I had always been the youngest sibling, so it was exciting to now meet a younger sister who was named after me. We had an amazing summer! They showed us pictures of ourselves that I never knew existed. We even listened to a cassette tape of Kim and me singing Christmas songs, she was four and a half, and I was one. It was really starting to sink in now... This incredible man really loves me as his daughter, a love I had never felt before.

Meeting them and learning for the first time the true stories of our childhood, and what had taken place that Friday afternoon, when my mom kidnapped us and drove us to Florida, was truly a gift and brought closure and answers to some of my biggest questions.

We continued to stay in touch. My brothers, who were a lot older when we lived in Arizona and had more vivid memories, especially of Chuy and his yellow pick-up truck, could not get on planes fast enough. It was truly a gift from the universe that we were back in each other's lives.

I was so blessed to grow up with two wonderful big brothers who took care of me and loved me in a very daughterly way, but I finally had Papa in my life again.

My relationship blossomed even more with Wanda, Chuy, and Kelly when I was stationed in Tucson during my time in the Air Force. Davis-Monthan Air Force base was only two hours away from Phoenix, and I made it a priority to visit my foster family on weekends. It was during these visits that I continued to learn about the first two years of my life, which was a huge gift.

And as I alluded to earlier... in July of 1989, only one month after Kelly's first marriage, Wanda and Chuy flew to Kalispell, Montana. Wearing the same tuxedo as he wore walking "Little Kelly," as she was now affectionately referred to, my first father, the one who loved me so much and lost me so tragically, was walking me down the aisle.

Our incredible story continues today. This year, Chuy turns 90 years old, and we are surprising him for Father's Day and flying out to Arizona once again. I am grateful to be able to celebrate the man who stepped in unconditionally and became my father... filling a place in my heart that could only be filled by him.

Terri L Trapp

Founder/Coach/Advocate

https://www.facebook.com/terri.trapp.trappteam.nwj
www.restorative-wealth.com
www.financial-wealth.com

Terri Trapp is a founder, advisor, coach, and advocate for holistic living, dedicated to empowering individuals and families to achieve financial freedom while prioritizing core values and family focus. As the principal advisor at Trapp Team-NWJ, a family-owned firm in Sussex County, NJ, powered by PFSI since 2007, Terri specializes in debt remediation, wealth-building, estate planning—including provisions for pets and businesses—and rebuilding life after loss. Her signature W.I.S.E. and P.A.T.H. programs emphasize financial self-care and recovery from life changes. Terri is deeply involved in community impact, supporting underserved groups, domestic abuse survivors, displaced families, and small businesses. She volunteers passionately for feral cat rescues and Collie adoptions. Alongside her husband Mark, she plays a Christmas Elf at the German Christmas Mart to raise funds for Sussex County charities. Terri is also an author and is committed to mentoring the next generation of women in her firm, ensuring a sustainable path to financial literacy and well-being. Her work focuses on impacting lives through educational materials, workshops, and coaching services designed to help people take control of their financial future.

Legacy in Action: Lessons Learned and Living One Percent Better Each Day

By Terri L Trapp

Dear Honored Grandfathers,

As I sit with pen in hand and heart wide open, I find myself reflecting on the extraordinary men who shaped the very core of my being. This chapter is for each of you—by blood, by marriage, by friendship, and by spirit. Your presence, your stories, and your lessons are the foundation upon which I have built my life, my work, my family, and my purpose. I write to honor you, to thank you, and to share how your legacy lives on, not just in me, but in every life I touch.

The Strength of Many: My Grandfather's Circle

Most people are lucky to have one or two grandfathers. I had a circle—a constellation of strong-willed, family-focused, and impactful men. Some were part of my life from the very beginning, others entered unexpectedly, and some I never met in person but felt through stories and shared blood. Each of you, in your own way, left indelible fingerprints on my heart.

Lessons in Service and Work: Grandpa Edgar

Grandpa Edgar, your influence is woven through every fiber of my professional life. You were a man of action and integrity, a quiet force for good in your community. I remember sitting on your porch, listening to your stories—not just of success, but of service. You helped neighbors keep their homes, guided friends through hard times, and always did what was right, even when no one was watching.

You taught me that a life of service is a life well-lived. When I chose my career in financial literacy and legal mastery, it was your example that gave me courage. The family didn't always understand my path, but your lesson—do what you need to follow the fingerprint on your soul—echoed in my heart. Today, my business is dedicated to educating and empowering others, offering a hand up, not a handout. Every workshop, every client, every moment spent helping someone build a better future is a tribute to you.

The Heart of the Homestead: Great Granddad Jesse

Great Granddad Jesse, your life on the homestead is a story I carry with pride. You were a self-sufficient farmer, a "goat man" whose herd saved countless babies during WWII when mothers joined the war effort. I can almost smell the fresh hay, hear the bleating of goats, and see your steady hands working in the early morning light. You taught me the rhythms of planting, the patience of growth, and the healing power of nature.

My passion for herbal remedies, gardening, and living close to the earth comes from you. Summers spent learning about animals and farm life taught me the daily

grind, the patience, and the resourcefulness needed to thrive when resources are scarce. Living off-grid, far from medical help or modern conveniences, meant making do with what you had and finding a way through. These lessons have served me well—on the trails of the Appalachian Mountains, during trips through the Rockies, and in every challenge life has thrown my way.

Compassion for All Creatures: Advocacy for Animals

Two of you, in particular, deepened my advocacy for animals. You showed me that compassion is not limited to people, and that our stewardship extends to all living things. Through your actions, I learned to speak for those who cannot speak for themselves, to protect and nurture, and to see the interconnectedness of all life.

Today, I support organizations like Friends of Ferals, helping to care for and protect vulnerable animals in our community. Whether it's volunteering, fundraising, or simply offering a safe haven to a stray, I am reminded of the gentle hands and kind hearts that taught me these values.

Family, Resilience, and the Power of Unconditional Love

My mother's fathers brought complexity and depth to my understanding of family. "Dad" Otis, your commitment to your promises and your word was unwavering. You loved your family unconditionally and lived each day as if it were your last. I will never forget our camping trips, blueberry picking, and cooking with you and Grandma Velma. Those memories are some of my happiest, full of laughter, adventure, and the quiet joy of being together in nature.

You were the first family death that truly shook my world. I was only ten, but the loss was profound. In your absence, I learned that love does not end with death; it transforms, becoming a guiding light that helps us find our way. Your lesson—to live fully, to cherish each moment, and to keep your word—remains at the heart of my family.

To my biological grandfather, Denni, whom I never met: Through stories and shared DNA, I learned that family is family, even if they are not present. Blood and history connect us, and for that, I am grateful.

Entrepreneurial Spirit and Community Leadership: Pap Pap

Pap Pap, my father's grandfather, embodied the entrepreneurial spirit. As a German man in a time of limited opportunity, you built a business, taught your sons trades, and ensured your family's survival. Your resilience and determination inspire me to serve my community through outreach and education, to be a center of influence, and to create opportunities for others.

Visiting Edgar's farm in Mahwah, seeing his passion for his greenhouses and his beloved dogs, are memories that live deep inside me. Each time I drive that direction for an event or workshop, I feel your presence, guiding my steps and reminding me to use my gifts for the betterment of the community.

The Rock of My Life: Grandpa Jimmie

And then, there is Grandpa Jimmie. Though not related by blood, you were my rock, my guiding star, and my greatest teacher. From you, I learned patriotism—not as blind allegiance, but as a deep love for country, family, and community. You taught me the meaning of sacrifice, the quiet strength of unending love, and the importance of being present, even after loss.

When you put on your pajamas at the age of 100 and said, "I did what I said I would, and now I want my Rosie," you taught me that a life well-lived is measured by love kept and promises fulfilled. Your solemn presence and aged wisdom seemed permanent, an unchanging facet of my world. I choose to remember the good, and by doing so, I recognize that you will truly never be gone; a mirror of the best traits a man can possess lives on every day in the shape of my son, who has placed his family's security at the forefront of his life, very much like you did.

You called me "Grace Bee Ace," reminding me that my kindness is a strength, not a weakness. You taught me that being busy as a bee is a virtue if it brings happiness, and that my passion for mastering unconventional things is a gift. When life knocked me down, you encouraged me to get up one more time, to try just a little bit harder, and to teach others what is possible. Our family motto, "Im omnia paratus"—I am ready for all—lives in me because of you.

Living the Lessons: My Life Today

Each of you left fingerprints on my heart that time cannot erase. Your laughter echoes in my happiest memories, and your advice guides me through my hardest days. Even in your absence, your love is a steady light that helps me find my way. I often catch myself repeating your words, realizing only now how wise you truly were. The lessons you taught me are the roots that keep me grounded and the wings that let me soar.

Though I can no longer hold your hand, I feel your presence in every act of kindness I offer to others. Your stories are the treasures I carry, sharing them with the next generation so your spirit lives on. You taught me that strength is not just in muscle, but in compassion, patience, and unwavering support.

I miss our talks, the warmth of your hugs, and the feeling that, no matter what, I was safe when you were near. Even now, I find myself reaching for the phone to share a story or seek your wisdom, only to remember you're no longer there to answer. But then I realize, you are still with me—in every lesson, every value, every act of kindness I extend to others.

Giving Back and Building Community

Your influence is visible in everything I do. My business is dedicated to lifting others up, providing education and resources to families facing hard times. I volunteer with organizations like Friends of Ferals, DASI, and local shelters, supporting children, families, and animals in need. Over the years, our home has been a refuge for young children and family friends who needed love and shelter—a living testament to the open-heartedness you modeled.

Our family's commitment to service continues through my sons. We spent years camping year-round, supporting them through Boy

Scouts, and celebrating their achievements as Eagle Scouts and leaders in the Order of the Arrow. The values of adventure, resourcefulness, and service you instilled in me are now part of their lives, too.

Resilience Through Adversity

Life has tested me in ways I could never have imagined. In the span of ten years, I survived a catastrophic fall, breaking my neck, shattering my spine and hip, and spending ten months in a drug-induced state 12–16 hours a day. The doctors said I shouldn't have made it, but the tenacity taught by Jesse and Otis, the love and dedication to my family like Jimmie, and the stubbornness of all my grandfathers somehow got me through.

Then, our home was hit by lightning and burned in a six-alarm fire. Ten days later, our youngest son was hit head-on by a drunk driver. Because of what you taught me, I was prepared—not just with insurance and business measures, but with the emotional strength to take the time he needed to recover. For ten months, we focused on his healing, only for tragedy to strike again when his body, too weak from the first accident, could not survive a second crash. He died before we could say goodbye.

In the depths of grief, I remembered the stories of Pap Pap, of sons lost in war, of Edgar losing his brother Myron over Poland. I learned that the only way forward is through, that love endures even when the heart is shattered, and that hope is not a plan, but persistence is.

Even as we grieved, life kept coming. A tick bite nearly took me from my family again, but the resolve and stubbornness learned from you kept me fighting. With no home, no toothbrush, and no bed, we trekked across state lines for treatment, just as **Jesse's family** had done on the Oregon Trail. My family, my clients, and my community were my "why" to endure.

One Percent Better, Every Day

If there is one lesson that ties all your wisdom together, it is this: live, live, live each day to the fullest, and strive to be one percent better and go one step further every day. The impossible becomes possible with just a bit more effort, a bit more hope, a bit more love.

You were the best grandfathers, great-grandfathers, mentors, guides, and friends a girl could ever ask for. I hurt so much because the love is so strong, with so many memories and so much love, I feel lost. I feel confused. Where does the love go now? To my husband and eldest son.

Your solemn presence and aged wisdom seemed permanent, an unchanging facet of my world. I choose to remember the good and by doing so, I recognize that you will truly never be gone; a mirror of the best traits a man can possess lives on every day in the shape of my son, who has placed family's security at the forefront of his life, very much like you did.

Carrying the Torch

Because of all of you, I am persistent, tenacious, and strong-willed. I love with grace, lead others through challenges, and in my business and career, shine a light of hope even in the darkest times. I am ready for all because I am committed to persevering, to serving, and to honoring your legacy.

Thank you for the lessons learned and the life changes made. I am who I am because of you, and I promise to carry your wisdom forward, helping others find their own strength, purpose, and hope. Your legacy is in action, every day, as I live, love, and strive to be just a little bit better, for myself, my family, and the world.

With unending love and gratitude,

Your Grandchild,
Terri "Grace Bee Ace"

Helene Su

Somatic Visionary Guide

https://www.linkedin.com/in/helene-su/
https://www.facebook.com/profile.php?id=61566169655329
https://www.instagram.com/helenesu.niiodance/
www.niiodance.com

Helene helps Heart-Centered Visionaries and Leaders reconnect to their True Self, Joy, Creativity and Power and is founder of Niio Dance for New Integrated and Inspired Openings. With a blend of +ve Psychology, plus the ancient wisdom of the East and the Indigenous, she gives you roadmaps for your body, mind and soul, through Embodied Creativity and Somatic Visioning. It has nothing to do with dance 'ability' or 'talent'. Instead find a deeper connection to your Inspired Self, the ego less Self that rises above self-judgement and self sabotage, infinite and powerful, Over the last 20 years she has given talks and workshops at festivals in the UK and Europe including the Conference in Dance and Spirituality and the Creative Summit for the World Arts and Embodiment Forum. She is a qualified yoga teacher, Reiki Master, studied Dance Movement Therapy and has an MA in Dance and Somatic Wellbeing.

The Man Who Gave Me Wings:
A Daughter's Tribute to a Legacy of Courage, Grace, and Grounded Strength

By Helene Su

The Departure
He Left So We Could Begin

My father was the most innocent, unassuming, trusting person I've ever known. If you asked him for something, he would simply say yes. Not out of passivity, but because he lived from a place of quiet selflessness. That was who he was.

He left Hong Kong in his early twenties—before it became the booming financial centre we know today. Back then, life was modest, uncertain. He was the eldest son, and with that came the unspoken but immovable weight of responsibility. So, he boarded a boat, bound for a foreign land. England. Cold, unknown, and full of unfamiliar customs and faces. But he went. Because family duty called.

He worked as a waiter, long hours on his feet, in a country where he barely spoke the language. And yet, from those wages, he sent money home. Enough to put his younger sister through college. He never boasted. He never asked for anything in return. That was just who he was.

The Quiet Strength
Lessons in Softness, Power, and Steady Presence

He never had the luxury of further education or leisure time until he retired. He worked. He provided. He got on with things. I never heard him complain about early mornings or aching legs. If a meal was mediocre, he'd still say it was okay. If life was hard, he bore it silently. My father was a peacemaker. A gentle soul with a bedrock spirit.

Growing up, he wasn't always physically present—work often took him away. But when he was home, I treasured those moments. Like the time he took me, just me, to see *Snow White*. I will always remember how the first supporting movie that came on scared the daylights out of me. It was about a father and son on a private plane that crashed in the desert. The boy was the sole survivor and was scratching around for food, encountering all kinds of strange and scary creatures. I was terrified that that could happen to me, and oh, how he laughed gently and teased me.

And although my mother was the louder voice in our home, it was my father whose quiet remarks carried weight. Because he was usually quiet, so when he spoke, I listened. Like the time when I told him I wanted to be a hairdresser (I was 16, had recently given up dancing, thinking I wasn't good enough to do it professionally, and still wanted to do something creative). Dad rarely voiced opinions, but when he said, "I can't believe you just want to be a hairdresser," I paused. Now, I had not wanted to be any old 'blue rinse' hairdresser but imagined working for Vidal Sassoon in London, those TV ads in the 1970s were very glamourous… but I changed course.

Similarly, when I didn't think I wanted to go to university, he reminded me, "I had to send money home so your aunties could study. You have this for free." His voice was steady, never guilt-laden, just truth. He was right, and go I did (I have, in fact, been to three universities!)

The Unspoken Legacy
How He Shaped Me Without Ever Saying a Word

From him, I learned that strength doesn't always roar. Sometimes, it simply endures. It boards boats. It sends money home. It walks through racism, exhaustion, and invisibility without ever asking to be seen.

He encouraged every adventure I ever dreamed of. He supported my wild ideas, my travels. And he was open-minded. I had gotten a tattoo whilst traveling, and I had been terrified to tell my parents. When I finally plucked up the courage to tell them, Dad's reaction was simply, 'Is it a butterfly?'

His quiet curiosity never faded. When I was planning a move to Brighton, my mother resisted, but Dad quietly said, "If that's what you want to do, go for it."

When I went traveling alone across continents, selling art on the streets of Tokyo, or considering moving cities, he never told me to stop. He gave me unspoken permission, perhaps because he recognized in me that same fire he once used to cross oceans. That same instinct to leap into the unknown.

Dad had a hidden adventurousness that not many would expect. In his sixties, I took him and my son Jyoti camping for the first time. We drove five hours to Cornwall with no campsite booked, and we ended up in a basic field with just a portaloo. And he did it. Cheerfully. If he struggled with the portaloo, he never said a word.

Mum didn't come because she worried about what people would think about someone her age camping. But Dad wasn't bothered by such things, and he came. He was up for it.

Later, in his sixties again, when I took Mum and Dad to Hawaii, I'll never forget the day we visited an inactive volcano. I went off to walk around its rim, and Dad just followed without me asking. I hadn't expected either of them to come, and sure enough, Mum was too frightened. But there, Dad wanted to explore with me. And so, we walked together, across ancient earth and black rock. Yes, that was my dad.

He was never showy, never loud, but there was a kind of quiet bravery to him that I only came to fully appreciate as I grew older. Whether it was boarding that boat or joining me in places far beyond his comfort zone, he always said yes when it mattered. He led by example: with quiet presence, with steady encouragement, and with an open heart.

The Inheritance and Gift
Carrying His Spirit Into My Dance, My Work, My World

It wasn't just that he came to the UK that I owed my Dad so much. It was what his decision made possible. His quiet courage shaped my entire life.

Because he got on that boat, I didn't risk my life protesting in the university student riots in Tiananmen Square, Beijing, in 1989, when innocent young people protested wanting more freedom and choice in their lives. I was at university myself at the time, but here in the UK. I watched the demonstrations and crackdowns against those young people with utter horror. Had I have grown up there, I would have been there in the crowd, without a doubt. As it was, I was safe watching on the TV, and I remember feeling so grateful for the comparative freedom I had here instead.

And that freedom—of movement, of expression, of presence—became the seed of my life's work. My movement practice. My offering to the world. I was free to explore. To dance. To express. To create, which is why I have created Niio Dance, a practice to empower you to stand up and own your unique brilliance, and express with creative freedom.

I especially support those who feel rootless or disconnected to find a home within themselves. Just like Dad must have felt, arriving in a land that did not speak his language and did not welcome him with open arms. But he endured. And I carry that memory in every breath, every step, and every dance.

Even as the world shifts beneath our feet, even as we navigate unstable leadership, disconnection, and rapid change, I think of the courage it took my dad to sail into the unknown. These days, we take flights in hours, we connect through screens, we carry worlds in our palms.

But back then, life was uncertain, risky and physical. And his choice—to leave, to begin anew—remains one of the bravest acts I know.

My dad's journey gave me the foundation to create a life of embodiment, movement, and creative freedom. It gave me the courage to reinvent myself time and again, to move countries, to start anew, to trust the unknown. That sense of internal grounding—of belonging in my body when the world feels uprooted—is something I now help others reclaim. And it's because of him.

The Quiet Goodbye
Honouring the Man Who Always Said Yes

Toward the end, Dad became quite frail. He would sometimes fall, but still, he avoided accepting help. He insisted on doing things himself. Until he simply couldn't anymore. Even then, he held onto his pride and his independence as long as he possibly could.

When I hear stories of absent fathers, I realize how lucky I've been. He wasn't always around, working such long hours away from home, but he stoically provided. He didn't always know how to show love in words, but his unspoken love was unwavering and palpable. He showed up. And he loved us in every silent gesture, every unseen sacrifice.

My father was too kind, my mother would say. He lent records to friends who returned them scratched, and he would never say a word. But that gentleness was his quiet power. His humility, his grace, his unshakable sense of duty. He didn't sweat the small stuff.

I am unbelievably grateful to my dad for his sacrifices. For his softness and his strength, and for the life he made possible for me, my sister and brother.

Because he boarded that boat all those years ago, I was given wings that can take me wherever I choose to go.

That is a gift that is priceless. The gift of freedom and possibility. And that is the gift that I now give to others through my craft.

Thank You, Dad, you are forever in my heart.

Janet Hamilton

CEO of The Anomaly Factor
International Life and Health Coach

https://www.linkedin.com/in/janet-hamilton-44054323
https://www.facebook.com/janet.hamilton.148
https://www.instagram.com/Janet10hams
http://www.theanomalyfactor.com
https://www.durhamcombustion.com

Janet is an Integrative Holistic Practitioner, Author, Podcaster and Speaker with 20 years of personal development experience. After a long journey of self-discovery, she has found inner peace and connection, realizing her uniqueness as an anomaly. Once feeling disconnected and burdened, Janet has aligned with her soul's purpose and is now living life to the fullest. Having learned the importance of self-love after years of neglecting herself, she became a self-love guru, breaking through limiting beliefs that held her back. Following a period of burnout and introspection, Janet created a podcast and website to share her insights and help others find their own calm and inner peace. Now residing by a serene lake, she enjoys a balanced life, surrounded by nature and supportive, like-minded individuals. Through her coaching business, Janet empowers others to discover their unique anomalies and embrace their authentic selves.

My Father, My Hero!

By Janet Hamilton

My father, Clark Joseph Allen, was born in Kinmount, Ontario, Canada, in 1941 to Irish descendants of the Peter Robinson settlers of 1825 from Ireland, my grandparents, James and Louise Allen (Pearson). My father shared the same birthday as his eldest brother who was eighteen years older to the day, there were three other boys and five girls in between. He came from a long lineage of lack and scarcity, with not a lot of money for even food at times.

My father came from a meager upbringing. His father had tuberculosis and was sent to the sanatorium in Hamilton when my father was three, and died when my father was only eleven; he really didn't know his father. His mom was from the Scottish Clan, the Pearsons. Both families settled in Galway, Ontario, many moons ago.

My grandmother ended up raising ten kids on her own as a single mom, left to run the farm and raise her children. My grandmother was very busy, and my Aunt Gerry, my father's eldest sister, ended up being more of a mother figure for him, who spoiled my father; she always had a soft spot for dad.

My father walked "five miles, barefoot in the snow," he would say, "with Kenny on my back." Kenny was born with club feet and was the first person that had them operated on at Sick Kids to remove and put on in the right direction. They were best friends right till the end, passing within a couple of years of each other.

My father was the youngest in his family and stayed back at the house to farm the land and look after his mother. He would work at the logging plant on Crystal Lake or run the horses near Salmon Lake when not working at home. He later worked at Canadian Tire, the gas bar (where he met my mother), doing truck deliveries, etc. My father was a very compassionate individual, always standing up for the underdog, what he believed to be right, etc.

My mom and dad met when my mom drove up to have her car gas tank filled, and my father was the man who pumped her gas. My mom obviously liked what she saw and drove around the block a couple of times so she could meet him. They later married in July of 1964. My mom and dad rented a basement apartment off a couple, who became lifelong friends and whom, at the time of this writing, I am still in contact with. They stayed there until after I was born, and they knew my younger brother was on his way.

After my brother was born in 1964, we moved to an apartment on Lawrence Avenue and where my dad started working for North York Hydro. He started out at Hydro working as a linesman and worked his way up to Supervisor of Operations. He did not apply for the job; They came to him and he had to negotiate his salary as he knew he made more working overtime and was protected by the union, he was well respected.

Four years later, when my sister was on her way, he bought his first house, washer, dryer, fridge, and stove, and he later told me he had just a few dollars left to his name after it all. We moved in, and he drove back and forth from North York to Oshawa to work. My father would often take on second jobs on top of his full-time job just to make ends meet. When we lived in the apartment, he would take me with him to clean offices, including our then-dentist, whom I had, long after I had my own kids, until he retired. My father cleaned his office so that he could get my teeth cleaned in exchange. After moving to Oshawa, he took on a job at a farm in Enniskillen as a farm hand. He would often work for twelve hours, drive home to Oshawa, and then have to sit at the kitchen table for hours on end due to outages, or whatever was going on at work.

My father was a big teacher and loved to educate us about life in general, how to be resourceful, how to make and save money, and he instilled in me values of family, honesty, integrity, and a strong work ethic. He told me if I was ever misfortunate enough to only have one piece of bread that I should share it with someone else. He was very political and fought to have the recycling of bottle program started when I was a young child in grade school, and he was a strong advocate for having the Park Road South bridge in Oshawa built. As young children walking to and from grade school, he didn't want us to have to cross the railroad tracks and thought it safer to go over and be protected. It didn't get built for many years later. He used to take me to the local town council meetings so that I could be exposed to how the political side of things worked.

My earliest recollection of spending time with my father was in the apartment; he would take my friends and me to the field track behind our apartment building and have us run races with each other around the track, which he then would pay the winner a quarter. I remember collecting garbage cans at the dentist's office and spending hours at the kitchen table cleaning and organizing coins and making waxed candles. Later, after moving to Oshawa, he would often pull my brother and me out of school to walk across the field, North of Bloor, and East of Park Road, to walk down to Lake Ontario and back again. At other times, he would drive us down to Camp X, which was also located on the shores of Lake Ontario, where the underground tunnels that they used to train the spies, such as the famous Intrepid, were still there. He would change the oil, and my brother and I would run the tunnels, playing hide and seek. He taught me finances so well that he used to borrow money from me when I was a young teenager, and when he couldn't pay me back when agreed upon, he taught me how to compound the interest, save for a rainy day, pay yourself first, etc. He also taught me not to borrow from friends or family and to look out for those around us who are misfortunate. He would inspect everything I was asked to do, my chores, and if they were not done to his expectations, I would have to do them over. He taught me how to change the oil and brakes in my car. On another occasion, he pulled my brother and me out of school to build the garage in the backyard. He would always say we would learn more doing whatever he had us doing, like building, than we would at school.

He and my mom divorced around the same time I got married, but had lived apart for many years prior. My father always looked after her, even after she had long left, either financially or by fixing things at her place.

In approximately the mid-1980s, my father had an angioplasty to unblock his artery that went bad, which ended up in a triple bypass instead, and he nearly lost his life. At the time, he was the second person to have the end piece of the angioplasty apparatus break off in his heart, three pieces that look like music notes. This was done at a famous hospital in Toronto. The next day, the surgeon was sitting on his bedside asking about a lawsuit, and my father said he had no intention of suing him. My father was awake for the whole surgery and knew what the doctor went through to save his life. Having said that, the surgeon also told my father and me that this had only ever happened once before, and they were able to get it out of the first person. He did not know what would happen, and told dad that he was a walking experiment; they were hoping that scar tissue would eventually build up around the three pieces and protect them from puncturing his heart; thirty-plus years later, and he was still kicking.

In 1994, my father had a heart attack and retired and moved back to his beloved hometown of Galway, in Kinmount. This is where he was born, raised, and wanted to die.

My father was known to many as "The Boss," and he would often even sign his notes to us that way. He had loads of charisma and was at times very funny; he was well respected, very analytical, and loved to have a good time. I don't recall my father drinking much except a couple of times, one of which was when his mom passed in 1979. He was quite the character, playing jokes, loving to laugh, absolutely loving Country music: his favorite artists were Johnny Cash, Loretta Lynn, Stompin' Tom Connors, Dolly Parton, Waylon Jennings, Charlie Rich, George Jones, and Willie Nelson, along with various others.

In approximately 2010, I started to care for my father as he had designated me to be his Power of Attorney for Personal Care, which I did for twelve years, after his diagnoses of Alzheimer's and dementia. This was an extremely hard time for me, physically and emotionally, and yet it was some of my fondest moments and memories of him. I got to know him on a completely different level, and then I was lucky enough to care for and protect him in his final years of life, like he had done for me for oh so many years.

Little did I realize who he really was until about two years after he passed. I learned, after completely burning out myself, that I was raised by my father, who was a narcissist. I was 58 years old when I learned this, and in hindsight, it made sense. I had always known that there were two sides to him, the one that I knew and the one that I knew not to know, to respect and never ask questions; this fear was also instilled in me from a very early age. I thought it was just normal parental respect and that that was just simply how things were.

My father taught me to be the strong, resilient, and independent woman that I am today. He taught me how to do research, to always stand up for what I believed in, and instilled a strong work ethic in me. He taught me that hard work, perseverance, discipline, and to trust a man at his word and usually on a handshake. He treated others how he wanted to be treated, but rarely was. People always thought they were taking advantage of him, and his attitude was that if they needed it worse than him, then let them have it; no one, and I do mean no one, ever pulled the wool over my father's eyes; he always knew what was going on.

I wish I knew what I know now, before his demise. Like my mother, he, too, grew up with childhood emotional neglect and being parentified; he was never allowed to be a kid, and as a result, I ended up being the same way.

He, like my mother, didn't know anything about love, even though they loved to the best of their capabilities.

When he died in March of 2022, I had him cremated and buried in the St. Patrick's Cemetery in his mother's place, where he wanted to be, and his headstone read, "I did it my way!" which he certainly did.

At my father's funeral, the last song I had played was his favorite song, it was sung by Mac Davis, "Oh Lord, It's Hard To Be Humble, When You Are Perfect In Everyway!"

Lastly, my father was not only my dad, and my hero, he was a great grandfather and my best friend whom I miss dearly but know he is with me, always! I love you dad!

Anna Barboza Lugo

Pure Tea Love & Women Inspiring Women and Men Too
Business Owner & Author

https://www.linkedin.com/in/anna-lugo-62746219/
https://www.facebook.com/@women.inspiring.women.2024
https://www.instagram.com/Alohalugo/
https://www.instagram.com/Up2uGod
https://www.puretealove.com/
https://women-inspiring-women-and-men-too.com/

Anna Barboza Lugo is a retired IT professional a single mother, a mentor, a business owner of a wellness company and a inspirational and spiritual leader. Her goal is to Inspire Leadership, Entrepreneurship, Mentorship, Fellowship, Worship, Friendships, Partnerships and Companionship through the She Wins Women's Network. Anna is also the Managing Partner for She Win's Women's Network in Las Vegas Nevada. She considers herself a prayer warrior, and a child of God.

Takes Someone Special To Be A Daddy!

By Anna Barboza Lugo

First of all, I want to acknowledge my Heavenly Father and Lord God for blessing me with two Dads, and a daddy for my daughter.

I remember very little about my birth daddy, but I do know one thing. Everyone called him Champ.

He most certainly was our champ in life. My daddy was a true veteran born on Veterans Day 11/11. When my daddy passed away, I was too young to understand death, I was too young to grasp the concept of what it meant to lose my dad. My dad served in the Army and suffered from a brain aneurysm. I was the youngest of four kids and my mom always assured me that my daddy loved being a dad to us four kids. When Daddy passed away, momma would have knell at our bedside to pray. I remember that I would always pray my daddy would come back home and bring me nickels. I don't know why nickels, I guess it was some sort of way to not feel broke. I truly believe my daddy has been my guardian angel watching over me from the day he arrived in heaven. If I could write a letter to my daddy, it would read something like this... "Dear Daddy, I know you have been with me in spirit, and I feel you have been my guardian angel since your death. I'm honored to be your Babygirl. I love that I get to be your daughter who stands humbled and proud of the Barboza name. I sure hope I make you proud in the humblest way. I am so thankful that I get to remember my roots.

In 1969, Momma met Papa Georgie, who would be the one person who selflessly gave his heart to a single mother with four kids. Once Mom decided that Papa Georgie would be her forever person, Pops moved us straight out of the projects to Redondo Beach. I was 10 years old and very happy to finally have a father figure in home and in our family. It was difficult living off Daddy's social security checks and we finally had someone who helped Mom run the home. Papa Georgie was the perfect blessing our family so desperately needed. He was our Hero and savior before we knew we needed one. He was someone who would love us unconditionally, be there when we needed a ride to school or if we needed help with homework: Pops was always happy to help. Papa became a grandpa to all our babies. They were his pride and joy. They were his most treasured human beings on the planet next to us four kids. He was the happiest when he was surrounded by his family. As long as he got his daily newspaper, cooked us BBQ, watched sports, and drank beer, he was happy. He taught me about all sports because he was a sports fanatic.

As Papa Georgie got older, he experienced dementia and Alzheimer's, a disease we knew little to nothing about. It would take his life, and it was at the end of his life that we witnessed Pops take his last breath. We showed him gratitude and told him he can go to heaven and be with his loved ones.

If I could write a letter to him, it would be as follows: "Dear Papa Georgie, Thank you for your selfless love. Your unconditional love was one constant in my life. I watched you pour everything you had into our family. There was a purpose that you came into our lives. To nurture us, to protect us, to help us grow into strong, confident, hardworking human beings like you. Thank you that you were our papa and second dad in my life. I often said if I ever marry, I want to marry someone just like you. Your love for our momma was truly a love so deep that it went even deeper and spilled onto us four kids. I most of all admired you for being not only a strong, hardworking man who committed his life to supporting us and providing our every need, but also for the pride you bore with your chest out when it came to supporting your grandchildren. You are most definitely the Hero of a Lifetime. I remember bringing my little three-pound baby girl, and you were afraid to hold her because you did not want to break her. You would always tease her and tell her we got her at the blue light special at Kmart. She was your little "shimp." You gave her that name because she could not pronounce shrimp and called it shimp, so she became your little shimp. You would be so proud of her. I love all our special moments, and this list is longer than possible. Every time and anytime I hear a Patsy Cline or George Strait song, I immediately think of you.

"Whenever I see your favorite Tina Turner movie, it reminds me of when I stayed the last night with you, and even though you were out of it, it was our last movie together. I also recall seeing a license plate on a car I parked next to at the hospital. It said MadPies; I truly believe it was a final message from you while here on Earth. I know that message had meaning behind it, because when we were younger, we would be giggling when we were supposed to be going to sleep.

"You would knock on our door and say, you Mag Pies better go to sleep or you're going to be tired in the morning. I truly believe these were messages to me that you knew I was there, staying by your side. I want to tell you that we miss you every single day. We were blessed that you came into our lives in 1969. God knew what he was doing when he brought you to us. Thank you for always lifting me up, wiping my tears, for all the car rides, and for buying us our first record player. The unconditional love was felt throughout, and I would not understand sports if it were not for you. I'm so glad you taught me football. I'm so grateful you gave me the strength to believe in myself. I am so thankful for all the many ways you made us feel like we were the most important people in your life. Thank you, George Earl Traver, for simply being the Best Pops ever!!

"Thank you for loving us like your very own. It takes a very Special person to be a Father, Dad, Pops, Gramps, and that was you, Pops. Thank you, thank you, thank you for being our Papa Georgie!!!"

I also want to write a letter to the man who stepped up and became a special man and father to my daughter. I've always said, "Any man can be a dad, but it takes someone truly special to be a father." I am beyond thankful that I met the man who would become my daughter's father. He is not her biological dad, but He is her ONLY dad and father figure who taught her to be herself, who taught her how to ride a bike and skateboard, who provided guidance, direction, and instilled the importance of education. He is her hero. After all, he was the one to save her behind a locked bathroom door, the first time he met her. It was cute that they met when he came to pick me up for our first date. I am beyond grateful, thankful, and blessed that her dad, even though he was her stepdad, was the one who stepped in and stepped up when the other stepped out. I'm truly grateful that even though our marriage did not work out, we still get to be friends and have our daughter's best interests at heart. Thank you, Leon Lugo, for being the Best Dad/Father a girl could ask for.

To all the Daddies, Dads, Papas, Pops, Stepdads, and Grandpas, thank you for being our greatest Heroes!!!

Rena McDonald

Founder of Eclipse Law Group

https://www.linkedin.com/in/rena-mcdonald-attorney-lasvegas/
https://www.facebook.com/rena.mcdonald.773
https://eclipselawgroup.com/

Rena McDonald is the managing partner of Eclipse Law Group, since its inception in 2007. A proud alumnus of the William S. Boyd School of Law, Rena earned her Juris Doctorate in 2003 and is licensed to practice in both Nevada State and Federal District Courts. Rena and her firm have garnered numerous accolades, including being named among the Top 100 Lawyers and Best of Las Vegas. She has also been recognized as a "person to know" in Southern Nevada. Her passion for making a difference extends from the courtroom to the community Born and raised in Las Vegas, Rena is deeply invested in her community. She sits on several boards for local charities and organizations. Rena is an International Best-Selling author and a dedicated mother of two.

Because I Never Say It

By Rena McDonald

I am going to start this message to Dads talking about my mother. My mother was everything to me growing up. She took care of me and made sure I was always able to try new things. She went to every concert and performance, every recital and every practice. My mother is an amazing woman who genuinely just wants to help everyone she meets. I know now that means she sometimes picks relationships with men who don't support her and with men who need help. Her kindness and generosity often led her to make choices that were not always in her best interest, but she always believed in the goodness of people and their potential to change. I hated watching what they put her through and how hard they made it for her.

My mom was enough, and I don't feel like I missed out, but I do know that her relationships left me feeling like I needed to be very independent and self-reliant. I thought I never needed anyone to be dependent on, as I never really felt that any man was going to reliably be someone I could count on or need. This independence shaped me into the person I am today, strong and capable, but it also left a void that I didn't realize was there until much later.

As I became a young woman and started dating, I found I was dating the same type of man my mother had been with. They all had issues and were incapable of providing me anything more than a project to "fix." After a particularly bad breakup, I realized this pattern and took some time to identify what I wanted. I spent time reflecting on my past relationships and understanding the reasons behind my choices. It was a journey of self-discovery and healing. Miraculously, when I declared to the world that I was ready to start looking again, I met you the next day. I wasn't sure about where it would lead, but I knew right away you were different.

Despite that, I treated you like every other guy that had ever been in my life. I was afraid to really trust you with anything. It was very hard to learn to trust you and be able to not only ask but rely on you for help. Our first pregnancy was very difficult and full of very stressful doctors' visits. Again and again, you supported me through my anxiety over the birth of our son. You always knew what to say. Your unwavering support and love during that time showed me that you were someone I could truly rely on. You were my rock, and I began to see that you were different from anyone I had ever known.

Our entire relationship, you have supported me when I needed it, whether I asked or not. More importantly, you made it okay for me to ask and know I could depend on you. I always wanted daughters because I knew I could raise them to be strong, amazing women. Life had other lessons for me when we were gifted with two amazing young men. I was so worried that I wouldn't be able to be what they needed as a father. Which clearly, I cannot nor am I supposed to be. I never needed to worry. You are the most amazing father. I love watching you cherish and care for our boys. Your patience, kindness, and dedication to our family are truly remarkable.

You are an amazing example of what a dad should be, which isn't that surprising when I see your dad and what a great guy he is. You volunteer and give up your weekends so that our boys can grow and do new things. You work hard to provide for our family. You are vulnerable and strong. I don't know how to teach these things to boys, but I don't have to because it is just part of who you are. Your ability to balance strength and vulnerability is something I deeply admire. You show our boys that it's okay to be both strong and sensitive, and that true strength comes from being authentic and caring.

You never let the boys win at chess or any other game. While I sometimes think you should, I do understand that it makes them try harder. When they do win, and they will, they will know they did it on their own, but with your encouragement and teaching. Those victories will be worth so much more. Your approach to parenting teaches them resilience and perseverance. They learn that success is earned through hard work and determination, and that the journey is just as important as the destination.

I am so proud of our boys and the example of a husband and father you have been to them. They will treat their spouses well, take care of their children, and keep your legacy of love and support alive by teaching their children to do the same. Your influence on their lives is immeasurable, and I am grateful for the role model you are to them.

I know you joke about how everyone knows me, and you let the spotlight shine on me. Some men would not be comfortable with letting me be successful. You support me so that I can be my best self, all while taking none of the credit. I listen to other women talk about their husbands' insecurities and struggles. I sometimes feel bad that I cannot relate. You have never made me feel bad about myself because I am doing well. That is a truly strong person who can lift others up in that way. Your selflessness and humility are qualities that make you truly special. You never seek recognition for your efforts, but your impact on our lives is profound. You are the foundation upon which our family stands, and your love and support enable us to thrive.

You should know that when we walk into a room and people are paying attention to me, you are the one I am watching. You are the one I care about. Your presence gives me confidence and strength. Knowing that you are by my side makes me feel invincible. You are my anchor, and I am grateful for your unwavering support.

That is not to say you are perfect; don't let this go to your head. Sometimes, you play video games too loudly or eat the last potato skin when I wanted it. But when push comes to shove, I know you are always in my corner and are always backing me up. You let me fight my own battles, but you are always ready to propel me forward if I start to falter. Your support is unwavering, and I know I can always count on you.

If we, as a family, stand tall, it is because you support us and lift us up on your broad shoulders. You are the greatest father and husband. I am thankful for everything you do and exactly who you are. Your love, strength, and dedication are the pillars of our family. You are my partner, my confidant, and my best friend. I am grateful for every moment we share and for the life we have built together.

Maria Magdalena Heinrich

Women's Informal Network Leader

https://www.linkedin.com/in/mariamagdalenaheinrich/

Maria Magdalena Heinrich is a wife and mother of three, a gender equality enthusiast, and part of the leadership team of the Women's Informal Network. Austrian by nationality, she was born in Rome, Italy, where she currently lives with her family. She studied Business Administration in Italy and the United States and, driven by a growth mindset, is continuously learning while traveling the world. Professionally, Maria Magdalena is a strategic planner who enjoys facilitating strategic planning discussions and incorporating risk management. She has proudly dedicated most of her career to the international development sector, striving to create a better world. In the Women's Informal Network, she runs the Informal Mentoring Programme and leads various initiatives to strengthen women's leadership. She also dances American Tribal Style Belly Dance, a group improvisational dance form where each woman is both a leader and a follower—just like in real life.

Your Life Was Your Message

By Maria Magdalena Heinrich

A letter to my father, Rudolf Heinrich (Ministerial Counsellor, Minister Plenipotentiary, Graduate Engineer, Doctor of Natural Sciences)

My Dearest Papa,

There is so much I wish I could say to you face-to-face. Since passing on 11 September 2024, not a day has gone by that I haven't thought of you, missed your voice, your guidance, and your solid presence in my life. This letter is my way of speaking to you, from daughter to father, from soul to soul. You lived an extraordinary life—one that continues to inspire me as well as other people, and I want to honor it by reflecting on the essence of who you were and how deeply you have shaped who I am.

I know that being born in Linz in 1941, during the turmoil of the Second World War, molded your worldview deeply. From a young age, you experienced the scarcity and fragility of life, and this forged in you a lifelong drive to build, to repair, and to contribute meaningfully to the world. It made you live in an austere and principled manner. You gave no value to brands or material status. Instead, you placed your highest regard in knowledge, faith, and the human spirit. That ethos guided everything you did—and everything you taught us to value.

You were the embodiment of a life lived fully, with purpose, where every day counted. The last time we spoke, you told me, *"Ich habe ein schönes Leben gehabt. Ich habe alles gemacht, was ich machen wollte."* — *"I had a beautiful life. I did everything I wanted to do."* Those words brought me immense comfort after passing; what a quiet triumph and a final gift. You never let a day go to waste. Whether traveling to remote corners of the world, mentoring young people, planting trees, or simply walking through the forest, you infused each moment with meaning. You taught me that when a decision must be made, we must make it—even when it's difficult. Procrastination had no place in your world.

From you, I learned to embrace life with courage. That lesson stays with me, Papa, guiding every decision I make. I face responsibilities head-on and strive to live with intention, just as you did. I welcome opportunities when they arise, trusting, like you believed, that where there is a will there is a way, there's a way. I try not to waste time on anything that doesn't move me or others forward.

In doing so, I also carry with me your deep joy for life, your love of skiing, tennis, and swimming; your delight in mushroom foraging in Weitensfeld and tending your garden in Casalpalocco. But above all, I remember your devotion to family.

Family was your greatest joy and your highest priority. You were deeply connected to us—Mama, Dominik, me and your sisters—as well as to your grandchildren, nieces, nephews, and extended family. You celebrated every milestone with pride, never missing a baptism, communion, confirmation, birthday, wedding, or ordination. You called regularly, offered advice freely, and always showed up. Whether organizing family gatherings, preparing the Christmas crib, or talking late into the night on the terrace, your love was unwavering and tireless.

You showed us the value of loyalty and the comfort of tradition. Your example taught me to care deeply, listen attentively, and make time for those I love. Our family was strong because of you—and your love continues to sustain us. Being together as a family was sacred to you. You placed great value on tradition, especially our Christmases in Linz with Tante Maria, Tante Christa, and their families. No matter where you had traveled or what responsibilities awaited, returning home for Christmas was non-negotiable. The joy of being together— sharing meals, stories, and laughter—bound us across generations. You believed those moments formed the fabric of who we are. You made sure we never forgot our roots, and you taught us to cherish and nurture them with love. That joy, that vibrant optimism, made you the heartbeat of our lives.

You were on a mission to make the world—and especially Europe—a better place. You never sought recognition; you acted out of principle and a deep sense of duty. It was clear that doing what was right mattered more to you than being acknowledged for it. And though recognition did come, it was never your goal. Your true purpose was always to serve and uplift—quietly, steadily, and with unwavering generosity.

Your extraordinary professional life has taught me the value of dedication and devotion and shown me how tireless effort and optimism can achieve incredible things. From the Federal Ministry of Agriculture, Forestry, Regions and Water Management to take the Austrian expertise to global levels, to an international career as a quiet and effective diplomat, weaving things together and making what seemed impossible happen.

Your commitment to the global cause of sustainable forest development left a lasting mark on policy and practice, working over three decades, in more than 170 countries, and collaborating with major global institutions.

Beyond your work in forestry and development, your deeper mission was to help shape a stronger Europe—culturally, spiritually, and morally, a united Europe, firmly anchored in its roots, where faith and culture would flourish once more.

I always admired how you devoted yourself to the formation of young minds, fostering dialogue across traditions and regions, and promoting the values of integrity, solidarity, and peace, and the student association Capitolina which you founded and led for over 35 years, lives on as an expression of your vision: to bridge nations and generations through the principles of faith, friendship, learning, and love for one's homeland.

Your generosity extended far beyond your profession. On every mission, you carried rosaries and religious materials, offering comfort to churches under pressure, donating your own resources to support projects in oppressed nations and standing firmly with those whose voices were silenced. You were always available—with advice, with action. From you, I learned that the greatest reward in doing good lies in knowing you have done your part. This lesson has become the foundation of my leadership, anchored in clarity, compassion and purpose. As leader of the Women's Informal Network, I strive to improve the world—not for praise, but rather because it is right. The network unites women in international development through mutual support, dialogue, knowledge sharing, and collective growth. Like you, I believe in the power of community to uplift others and in upholding shared values across nations.

Though you never sought recognition, your integrity did not go unnoticed. I was so proud when you were awarded the Grand Decoration of Honour for Services to the Republic of Austria and the Order of St. Sylvester from the Vatican tributes to the values that defined your life.

Your legacy lives on—in the churches you supported, the priests you mentored, and the enduring vision of a spiritually rooted, united Europe that you helped keep alive.

Your many affiliations reflected a life rooted in deep faith, civic engagement, and professional excellence. From your active roles in Catholic organizations and student fraternities in Vienna, Rome, and Prague, to your leadership in international forestry bodies and your commitment to the Austrian communities abroad, you lived your values with consistency and purpose. Your example inspired me and many others to seek meaning not just in personal success, but in contributing to something larger than myself—faith, community, and service.

You were a generous husband, father, and grandfather who left a lasting mark on our family. Papa, your voice was unmistakable—honest, direct, and often disarming to those unprepared for such candor. You spoke with conviction, sometimes sharply, driven by a belief that truth should never be hidden behind politeness when something truly mattered. You would have appreciated Pope Leo XIV's recent message, in which he emphasized that truthful communication is essential for building genuine peace and authentic relationships. He reminded us that truth is not grounded in abstract principles, but in love, a sense of responsibility for others, and the living encounter with Christ—empowering us to face today's global challenges with clarity and compassion.

One moment I now remember with a smile is the speech you gave at my wedding as the father of the bride. Instead of focusing solely on personal anecdotes or emotional blessings, you chose to speak about your concern for the unity of Europe as well as the preservation of our Christian cultural heritage. At first, I was surprised and, if I am honest, even a bit upset—after all, it was my wedding day, and I had hoped for a more personal touch. Now, 21 years later, with everything happening geopolitically in Europe and beyond, I can see so clearly what you were doing. You were using that moment, with a young and attentive audience before you, to deliver a heartfelt appeal to protect what truly mattered to you. That moment has grown in meaning for me over time, becoming yet another testament to how deeply your convictions shaped every word you spoke and every action you took.

You held strong opinions and rarely wavered, speaking with such certainty that it often left little room for other perspectives. Not out of disregard, but from a deep confidence in your values. That clarity, while sometimes challenging, carried its own integrity.

From you, I learned the importance of balancing honesty with empathy. Having felt the sharp edge of your words and seen their impact on others, I became more attuned to the emotions behind each exchange. You taught me that truth matters—but so does how it's spoken and how it lands.

And yet, for all your clarity and candor, you never told me outright that you were proud of me—not during my years of study, nor in my hobbies as a dancer or theatre actress, not for my professional career. That silence lingered.

That's why the moment you became a fan of my first book, *YOU MATTER – How Women Reclaiming Their Power Are Changing the World*, meant so much. When it was published in 2021, something shifted. For the first time, you openly expressed admiration for what I had done—and at that moment, I felt your pride.

You may not have said it often, but that rare affirmation echoed more loudly than words ever could. It reached a place in me that had long been waiting to be seen. It mattered more than you could have known.

Your optimism was your compass. Even in the face of illness, betrayal, and fatigue, you kept your eyes on the future. I saw how you endured your last years with immense discipline, confidence in God, and serenity. Despite the hurt inflicted by some whom you had helped the most, you did not grow bitter and kept to your mission because you believed in the greater cause, even if some individuals were unworthy. You showed us that personal disappointments must never distract from higher goals.

These last four years were a gift—earned through your discipline, your resilience, and your trust in God. You made the most of this time, continuing to give, to support, to believe. You never gave up. Not once.

Your example has taught me to keep my mind focused on what truly matters. I do not let obstacles shake me. I stay positive, because that's how you lived. That's how you led. And in my work, in my friendships, in how I raise my children, I try to reflect that same spirit of hope, strength, and dedication.

You and Mama—your wife for 58 years—built something beautiful. Your love was visible in everything you did together. Mama's strength and devotion mirrored yours. Together, you gave us roots and the strength to grow and bloom.

As your friend, Pope Benedict XVI, said: "The world offers you comfort. You were not made for comfort. You were made for greatness." Papa, you were made for greatness. And you lived up to it in every way.

Your final wish was fulfilled—you were laid to rest near the tomb of Saint Peter in the Vatican, under the orange tree you had chosen. I was deeply touched when more than 200 people from embassies, fraternities, churches, and communities around the world gathered to say goodbye and honor the man you were and the life you led with purpose and faith. I am grateful you are close by, so I can come speak with you and feel your presence whenever I need to.

I know that you are at peace now—and your light lives on in all of us.

Dearest Papa, your life was your message. I carry it with me every day, letting love lead—always.

With all my love,
Your daughter,
Maria Magdalena (aka Marilena)

Dr Rudolf Heinrich and Maria Magdalena Heinrich
at the First Communion Party on their terrace in Rome, 1986

Johanna Magdalena Posi

Johanna Magdalena Posi is an 11-year-old girl living in Rome with her family. The youngest of three siblings, she has an older sister, Christine, and a brother, Klaus. Johanna shares her family's love for travel and speaks both Italian and German fluently, reflecting her Italian and Austrian roots. She attends the German School of Rome, where her curiosity and creativity thrive. Johanna dreams of becoming a lawyer one day to defend people's rights, but she also has a deep passion for fashion. In her spare time, she loves designing and making her own clothes, imagining every detail with care and originality. She's also very sporty and trains regularly for triathlons, enjoying the challenges of swimming, cycling, and running. Through sport, fashion, and her studies, Johanna expresses herself with energy, imagination, and determination in everything she does.

All That You Are to Me, Dad

By Johanna Magdalena Posi

Dear Dad,

I didn't quite know where to begin. I thought about all the beautiful things you've done for me, and it occurred to me that I want everyone to know what an amazing father you are. I've always felt you were different, special, even if, as a child, I couldn't explain why. Over time, I understood you've always explained things to me in your own way. Not like everyone else does, but in a way only you can. And even when I got upset about a punishment or a decision I didn't like, deep down I knew you were doing it for my own good.

When I think of you, so many adjectives come to mind that describe you perfectly.

You are **patient** because even when I make the same mistake a thousand times—like with the dishwasher or when I forget something—you never lose your temper. You show me how to do it properly, explain why it matters, and you know that getting angry won't help, so you choose to teach me calmly. And I love that. Because that's how I really learn.

You are **loving** because every morning before I go to school, you give me a hug or a gentle touch on the head, and it's clear you do it with your whole heart. It's never rushed; it's always full of warmth, as if in that moment you want to pass on all the strength and calm, I need to face the day. Sometimes, you add a sweet phrase, a joke, or even just a quiet smile, but I feel it: It's your way of saying "I love you" without needing many words. Even when you're tired or have a million things on your mind, you never forget that gesture, and I wait for it—because it makes me feel important, protected, and loved. And it's not just in the morning: Your love shows up in a thousand little acts, like when you cover me if I fall asleep on the couch, or when you always remember to buy my favorite chocolate. It's that silent but steady love that follows me every day, even when I don't say it out loud.

You are **funny** because you always know how to make me laugh, even when I'm sad or nervous, maybe with one of your jokes. You always have something to talk or laugh about, and it's amazing how you can find the funny side of any situation. Your ability to lighten the mood with your sense of humor is unique, and you always lift my spirits with your words, making every worry fade away.

You are **romantic** because when you go out for dinner with Mom, you still plan little surprises, even though you've been married for so many years. You don't just pick any restaurant, but always look for beautiful, special places, the kind that creates a magical, unforgettable atmosphere. You explore the best places, with refined menus and cozy vibes, making sure every evening is perfect. On top of the dinner, you add small details to make it even more special, maybe a quiet spot for a walk afterward or a hidden place with a breathtaking view. Your attention to detail and your effort to make every moment with her unique are what make your love so extraordinary.

You are **creative** because you come up with brilliant solutions even in the most chaotic situations, like that time the car tire blew out on the highway on our way back from vacation. Instead of panicking, you stayed calm and found a solution right away. We called a tow truck, and it brought us to a town we had never heard of. It could have been just a forced stop, an annoying delay to forget—but instead, you turned it into something special. You found us a place to eat, made us laugh despite the tiredness, and turned that afternoon into a surprising little adventure. That town, which was once just an unexpected detour, has become one of the places we love to return to—a small emotional haven, full of memories. That's your strength: turning setbacks into opportunities, problems into beautiful memories. And you do it with such natural creativity that we always feel safe and full of gratitude.

You are **generous** because you always share everything with us—your time, your attention, even your things, even when you're tired or could use a moment for yourself. I admire the way you do things, the heart you put into them, and the reasons behind them. When I see you at your desk, on your computer, planning trips and vacations, I know you're not doing it just for you. In fact, you do it mostly for us. You want us to be well, to have fun, to live amazing experiences. And that generosity, that quiet dedication of yours, always touches me deeply.

You are **selfless** because you always care about others—even if you don't know them well—whether it's a neighbor, a colleague, or a friend of a friend. Your heart opens easily to anyone, and you never draw a line between someone you've known forever and someone you just met. Your ability to put yourself in others' shoes is extraordinary. You sense when someone needs a comforting word, a kind gesture, or a helping hand. No matter how small the issue is, you always find a way to help—offering support, listening, and advice. Your willingness to give without expecting anything in return stands out to everyone around you. Every time someone is in trouble, you are the first to step forward, trying to make a difference with your generous spirit and empathy. In a world that sometimes seems indifferent, your care for others is a true force for good—an example of how selflessness can change lives.

You are a **traveler** because you love discovering the world and always take us with you, showing us new places and teaching us to look with curious eyes. Every trip you take is a new adventure, a chance to explore different cultures, diving into traditions and landscapes we never imagined. It's not just about seeing places but experiencing them—soaking in the atmosphere and appreciating every detail. You bring us along for the ride, showing us not just the famous sights but also the hidden gems, the tucked-away spots only a true traveler would notice. With you, every journey becomes a chance to learn, to see the world in a new way, and to understand how fascinating and diverse life really is. Your love for travel isn't just a personal passion, it's an invitation to embrace the world with endless curiosity and to welcome every experience life offers.

You are a true **planner** because every vacation, every weekend, every detail is carefully thought out by you to make sure everything goes smoothly. You leave nothing to chance, and every part of our time together is designed with care so that every moment is special and stress-free. Each destination is chosen with purpose, every activity meant to entertain and relax all of us, and you try to include comfort to make us all happy. Even when you come home tired, instead of relaxing, you sit down to plan the next great moment we'll share. It's amazing how your energy and commitment never run out—always focused on creating new experiences together. This shows how much you care about making us feel loved and special. Your happiness is seeing us smile and enjoy every minute together. And that fills my heart, because it shows not only your dedication to us, but also your talent for turning every little occasion into an unforgettable memory.

And finally, you are **playful** because you still know how to have fun like a kid—whether it's a board game, a true crime story, or even a simple game of memory, you always create moments of joy.

You taught me that before acting, you must think—and that lesson helped you in your work, too, where you are a leader who leads by example and takes care of people. You're a real manager, in every sense: organized, dependable, empathetic, fair. You know how to make tough decisions when needed, always with respect for those around you. You truly listen—not just to respond, but to understand. You know how to motivate your team, make them feel valued, part of something greater. You make sure everyone has the right tools to work well and peacefully. You can foresee challenges and solve problems before they even arise. And most of all, you never put yourself above others—you're always ready to roll up your sleeves, help out, be present. Anyone who works with you knows they can rely on you.

Your leadership goes beyond your own team. Even those who work with you externally—partners, collaborators, clients—notice it immediately. They respect you because you are serious, competent, and consistently reliable. They admire you because you listen to their needs, find practical solutions, and keep your promises. People trust you, and it's no coincidence that anyone who works with you once wants to work with you again. Your professionalism, combined with your humanity, leaves a lasting positive impression in every relationship. And by watching you, I've learned what it means to be a true leader.

When I argue with my brother, you're always there. You don't jump to conclusions or take sides right away. You ask what happened, you listen, you think—and then you resolve. Calmly, fairly, lovingly. I really appreciate everything you do for us. Every time we go somewhere, I thank you right away, because I know how much time and effort you put into organizing everything perfectly, so we can enjoy those moments together.

You have a special gift: You always know what to say, when to say it, and how to say it. I've always admired you for that. I try, but I still don't know how you do it. You have calmness and clarity that are rare. It's like everything is already in order in your head. You think— and then say exactly the right thing, the thing that helps. It is not just intelligence or logic, it is your sensitivity that makes your words so precious. You can sense how someone is feeling without them saying a word. You know when comfort is needed, when silence is better, or when just one word is enough to make someone feel seen, heard, and welcomed. Your sensitivity isn't loud, it isn't showy; it's deep, quiet, and attentive. And because of that, it has an incredible impact.

And then... How do you find time for everything? You juggle work, plan, keep our home running, make time to play with me, stay strong through exercise, and care for everyone with love. It is important to you that my siblings and I grow up surrounded by love, with balance and inspired by strong role models. And you are our greatest role model of all.

I love you, Dad. So much. And I'm proud to be your daughter.

With love,
Johanna

Johanna Posi with her Dad, Andrea Posi during a trip just the two of them, 2025.

Wendy Raven Johnson

Founder of Designed To Be HER

https://www.facebook.com/groups/designedtobeher
https://www.instagram.com/wendyravenjohnson/
https://designedtobeher.com/
https://designedtobeher.com/report

Raven is The Identity Disruptor — a clinically trained Registered Nurse turned transformational guide for high-achieving women who feel successful on the outside but stuck on the inside. She is the founder of Designed to Be HER™: The Frequency Mirror™, a movement built on The Mirror. The Map. The Movement™. Raven helps women decode their true energetic blueprint so they can stop performing identities that were never theirs—and finally come home to the truth that always was. Her work bridges the seen and the unseen, using Human Design as the most precise method to make the invisible undeniable. Through her writing, message, and presence, she reflects truth without judgment and power without pressure. Her father's quiet strength didn't just influence her—it revealed her. His legacy lives in every mirror she now holds for others. Because of him, she remembered. Because of him, she became HER.

Because of You, I Am HER

By Wendy Raven Johnson

The Last Words That Shaped Me

"The strongest parts of me were shaped by the quiet strength of a man who never needed to say much—because his presence said it all."
~Wendy "Raven" Johnson

I can still hear his voice.
Rough, raw, and softened only for me.

"Princess," he'd say, like it was a full sentence—a comfort, a joke, and a love letter, all at once.

The day the ambulance came, the air shifted.
Heavy.
Thick with everything we didn't want to say.

I watched him reach out—not with the kind of strength he was known for, but with something deeper. I held his hand. And my whole world slipped through the cracks in that moment like gravel under the tires of his old truck.

"You're strong," he said. "Stronger than you know. Don't forget that. I love you. Never lose your strength"

That was the last thing he ever said to me.

I wanted to scream, *"You can't leave me. I need you. Who will be there for me now?"*
But I didn't. I just nodded.
Because I was trying to be strong—just like he taught me.

That was the day I faced a mirror I didn't ask to see.
Not the kind that hangs on a wall...

But the kind that reflects who you really are when the one person who made you feel safe in this world is being taken away.

That moment cracked me open.
It didn't break me.
It revealed me.
And because of him, I would never see myself the same again.

My Father, My Forever North Star

"I didn't just lose my father. I gained a compass I carry in my soul—the man who taught me to ride a snowmobile, a boat,
and eventually... my own truth."
~Wendy "Raven" Johnson

Most little girls look up to their fathers as heroes.
But mine... mine wasn't just my hero.
He was my compass.

From the moment I could walk, I followed his footsteps—into bait shops, onto frozen lakes, and into dusty trucks filled with the sound of old country songs and stories only he could tell.
I'd groan at his off-key singing, but now? That music plays like a memory, reminding me who I am and where I come from.

He was tough on the outside, but soft in all the places that mattered.
He grumbled about the dogs being underfoot while secretly slipping them treats under the table.
He cussed like a trucker, worked like a machine, and loved with a loyalty that never wavered.

He called me "Ellie May," not just for my love of animals, but because I never fit into the world's neat little box.
And the truth is—he loved that about me.
He saw my untamed, full-hearted nature and never once asked me to tone it down.

He didn't have an easy life.
Born in Port Arthur.
Placed for adoption.
Lied about his age to join the army at fifteen—not because he was reckless, but because he was searching for something: belonging, identity, purpose.

He took whatever job he had to—milk truck driver, coach bus operator, and eventually, cement truck driver. His work ethic showed up before the sun rose and didn't quit until long after it set.

In the winters, he and my mom ran an ice fishing business—up at 4 AM to ready the huts, ferry customers across the lake, and close it all down again at night. Day after day. Year after year.

He never complained. He showed up.
And somehow, even with the weight he carried, he always made space for me.

I was his Princess. His shadow.
If he went to the corner store, I went too.
If he went hunting or fishing, I was right beside him—tangled in rods and boots and love.

He taught me to drive a boat. A snowmobile.
And eventually... myself.

He showed me that love isn't about what you say—it's about where you stand when things get hard.
He stood beside me.
Every heartbreak. Every mistake. Every version of me.

He didn't ask for perfection.
He just asked me to be *me*—even when I forgot how.

He beamed with pride when I became a nurse. A mother. A woman who got back up every time life tried to break her.

He didn't always say the words, but I saw it in his eyes:
Pride.
Respect.
Unshakable love.

That's the thing about men like my father.
They speak with their presence more than their words. But when they do speak... You never forget it.

Love That Lingers Like Flannel

"Some inheritances come in dollars. Mine came in grit, grace, and the quiet kind of strength."
~Wendy "Raven" Johnson

Grief didn't come crashing in.
It arrived like his old flannel shirts in the laundry—soft, unraveling at the seams, but filled with the warmth of memory.

At first, it was the absence.
The missing footsteps.
The radio no longer crackling with country music.
The coffee cup that no longer held Bud Light.
The trip to the lake he never made.

The way I still caught myself looking up when I walked into a room—expecting to see him there.

But beneath the ache...
There was something else growing.
Something that didn't leave when he did.

He didn't leave me empty.
He left me *anchored*.

I didn't inherit his voice (God knows I didn't get his singing).
But I inherited his presence.

His resilience.

His "show up, no matter what" energy.

His belief that even when life knocks you sideways, you stand anyway.

He left me the kind of strength you don't post about.

You carry it.

You *become* it.

The kind of strength you tattoo on your wrist.

So you never forget who the hell you are.

After he passed, I did just that.

A simple word—*Strength*—inked onto my left wrist.

A promise. A reminder.

Whenever life starts to wobble, I run my thumb across it and remember:

He's still here.

In my grit.

In my grounded, unshakable *"I've got this"* energy.

He raised me to be strong.

Not just when it was convenient.

But when it was *crushing*.

And that strength didn't start with me.

It started with him.

How Loss Became My Life's Message

> *"The HER Identity isn't something I created. It's something I remembered—because he never let me forget."*
> ~Wendy "Raven" Johnson

You think the grief will wreck you.

And for a while, it does.

It's not always loud.
Sometimes, it's in the quiet.
The space between breaths.
The way you reach for the phone... and remember there's no one on the other end anymore.
The way you hear their voice—not out loud, but in your bones.

But eventually...
That ache starts to speak.

Not in his voice.
But in mine.

At first, I thought I was losing everything.
But grief—real grief—is just love with no place to go.
So, I gave it a direction.
I gave it a name.
I turned it into something that could outlive both of us.

It shows up in the way I love my kids—steady, stubborn, and soft where it matters.

It lives in the way I stopped performing for approval, and started walking in the truth of who I've always been.

What I thought was the end of his story...
Became the beginning of mine.

He didn't just leave me with memories.
He left me with a way of *being*.
A way of showing up.
A way of loving, leading, and living that doesn't require permission—only presence.

And every time I guide a woman through her own storm, every time I help her see herself in the mirror again— I see him.

I see the man who showed me that strength doesn't always roar.
Sometimes, it shows up with calloused hands and a soft heart.

Sometimes, it smells like old flannel and cigarette smoke.
Sometimes, it holds your hand before the ambulance doors close...
and reminds you:

You're stronger than you know.

That legacy?
It didn't die with him.
It lives in me.
And now, through me, it lives in those around me.

Becoming HER

"Identity isn't a performance. It's a remembering."
~Wendy "Raven" Johnson

I had a calling to help other women see what I did... HER.
I started this work because of a man who loved me
unconditionally—flaws and all— looked me in the eyes one last
time and said:
"You're strong. Stronger than you know. Don't forget that."

And I didn't.

Because I couldn't.
Those words weren't just his goodbye.
They were my beginning.

I knew there were women—so many women—who'd never had
anyone look them in the eyes and say that.
Who were waiting for proof before they claimed their power.
Who were performing roles instead of living truth.
Who forgot who they are.

So, I built something I wish every woman could have heard growing
up.

Not a blueprint.

Not a brand.
A **remembrance**.

Of softness as strength.
Of truth as liberation.
Of identity not as performance—but as **birthright**.

Because I watched a man who lost everything—his wife, his health—still show up for his daughter with love in one hand and legacy in the other.
And from him, I learned:
You don't have to be loud to be powerful.
You don't have to have it all together to lead.
You just have to show up... as you.

That's what *Designed to Be HER:The Frequency Mirror™* was born from.

Not a business.
A heartbeat.

A reflection.
A map.
A movement.

It's what happens when a woman stops chasing alignment—and starts moving as alignment.

It's what happens when she looks in the mirror, wipes away the world's expectations, and finally sees herself again.

Because when she does?
She doesn't just reclaim her confidence.
She **remembers her frequency**.

She stops apologizing.
She stops shrinking.
And she becomes HER.

To the Man Who Saw Me First

"You saw me long before the world ever did—and now,
I help others see themselves."
~Wendy "Raven" Johnson

Final Reflections—A Letter to My Dad

Because of You, I Am HER

Dear Dad,

There isn't a day that passes that I don't feel you.

In a song I once rolled my eyes at... now playing on repeat.
In the quiet of early mornings—when the world is still and strength feels sacred.
In the way I lead.
In the way I hold space for women to rise.

You were never loud about your love, but I never once doubted it.
Because you didn't show it in words.
You showed it in presence.

And now... Your love echoes in everything I do.
In every woman I hold a mirror to—when she's forgotten who she is.
In every whisper of truth I speak—when the world's been too loud for too long.
In every moment, I help her remember the HER she's always been.

You taught me that real strength isn't in the noise.
It's in the knowing.
It's in the staying.
It's in holding the line, especially when the world wants you to let go.

I carry that kind of strength now.

In my bones.
On my wrist.
And in every word I speak into the hearts of women.

You didn't just raise a daughter.
You raised a mirror.
A disruptor.
A legacy in motion.

And when I look in the mirror now... I see HER.
Because you saw me first.

I love you,
Forever your Princess ♡

* * *

Author Note: The Legacy Continues

This chapter isn't just a loving memory of my father.

It's a mirror for every woman who's ever needed to remember who she is.
Not through the noise of the world... But through the steady whisper of someone who truly *saw* her.

My dad may be gone, but his legacy lives on.
Not just in memory.
But in movement.
In the mission I now carry.
In the women I guide—through the Mirror, the Map, and the Movement™—as they meet the version of themselves that's always been there, waiting.

This is what I was designed for.
This is what I help her reclaim:
Strength. Identity. HER.

This isn't an ending.

It's a return.
It's a reckoning.
It's the beginning of HER.

Designed to be HER™. The Frequency Mirror™.

And every time I look in that mirror...
I remember.

Thanks, Dad.

XOXO
Wendy

Evelina Solís

CIO of Sol2Soul and Shine Your Light Christian Youth Camp and Programs, Co-Founder of Kingdom Youth Legacy, 5 Times Best-Selling Author, Inspirational Speaker, Certified Youth and Adult Transformational Empowerment Coach

https://linktr.ee/EvelinaSolis

Evelina Solís is an unstoppable powerhouse—a storyteller, inspirator, and joyful spirit with a heart as big as her love for tacos and Texas. As CEO of Sol2Soul and Shine Your Light Christian Youth Camps and Programs, and Co-founder of Kingdom Youth Legacy, Evelina lights up every room with her infectious energy, empowering both youth and adults to embrace their God-given gifts. After triumphing over a battle with Lupus, Evelina became a champion for those facing Lupus, PTSD, and neurodivergent children. Her mission is to help others shine brightly and live a purposeful life with unshakable faith. When she's not speaking, coaching or leading dynamic youth workshops, Evelina is cherishing memories with her daughter, Hope, traveling, enjoying the arts, playing sports or serving her church and community. She thrives on fiestas, food and laughter with her family and friends. Shine your light together by connecting with her at www.linktr.ee/EvelinaSolis.

Not Too Bad for a Little Mexican from La Grulla: My Father's Legacy of Faith, Family, Love, and Hard Work

By Evelina Solís

"Earthly fathers are a reflection of our Heavenly Father. When they love, sacrifice, and lead, they point us to God's enduring care."
— Unknown

A father's love is one of God's most profound gifts. It reflects His loving care and compassion. My dad's life is a living testament to how faith, grit, and sacrifice can shape a family's legacy. His journey wasn't easy, but his steadfast spirit and commitment to building a better future remind me of how God the Father nurtures, guides, and protects His children.

My dad's story begins in two small, humble towns, La Grulla, Texas, near the Mexican border, and Hoopeston, Illinois, nestled in the heart of the Midwest. As the eldest of seven siblings, he grew up quickly. From a young age, he carried the heavy weight of responsibility, laboring under the scorching sun as a migrant worker picking asparagus and detasseling corn in the fields. He was more than just a big brother, he was a steady role model, a quiet protector, and a constant provider. Even when resources were scarce, he made sure the younger ones, his hermanos and primos, had what they needed, often sacrificing his own comfort for theirs.

My dad was a standout student, sharp, hardworking, and relentlessly driven. His parents bussed him to a private school in a neighboring town to give him access to a better education and a brighter future. He rose to the top of his class, earning the title of Valedictorian in eighth grade, even surpassing the principal's own child.

As high school graduation neared, doors began to open like scholarships and opportunities. My dad's dreams were finally within reach, but just as his path was beginning to unfold, life intervened. His little sister got sick so he stayed back to help his family with the bills. Then, he was drafted at the end of the Vietnam war. Without hesitation, he set aside his personal ambitions to serve his country, answering the call with courage and honor. He taught us that success doesn't always follow a straight path; sometimes, we take detours and face challenges that require resilience to keep moving forward.

He didn't just put his dreams on hold, he laid them down. That choice defines the kind of man he is: brave and selfless, a true soldier, a true hero.

After my dad's military assignment was up and he came back to Hoopeston, he reunited with my mom, whom he met years earlier at a cousin's Quinceañera. This year marks 48 years of marriage, a testament to their enduring love, faith, and commitment. Their bond, grounded in prayer and God's word, has weathered life's storms and inspired us all.

Despite his own hardships, my dad remained committed to his faith and family. He knew God had a greater purpose for his life, even when the road seemed uncertain. This faith didn't just shape him; it shaped our entire family.

My parents' love story is my favorite. They married when my mom was 18 and my dad was 24. My dad's deep devotion to my mom has shown me that love is not just a feeling, but a daily choice, a covenant with God. They've built a beautiful legacy together and modeled the kind of marriage I hope to have one day.

Growing up, my dad always stressed the importance of education, saying, "Mija, échale ganas en la escuela para que no tengas que batallar como yo. Quiero que tengas una vida mejor." He didn't want his kids to face the same struggles he did growing up. He wanted us to maintain good grades in school so we could have a better life. He always made it clear that education was our ticket to a better future.

To teach my older brother and I the value of hard work, he allowed us to work with him at General Motors during our college summers. He knew that experiencing the hot, dirty, and tough conditions of manual labor would motivate us to finish a college degree. He never wanted us to settle for less, only for God's best. I'm so grateful for his guidance and wisdom all these years.

Through his hard work and perseverance, my dad ensured that all three of his children became the first in our immediate family to graduate from college. He didn't just push us academically; he encouraged us to dream big and pursue our goals without fear. For him, it wasn't just about building a career, it was about building Godly character and using our opportunities to make a difference in our school, church, and community. My dad and mom are always our biggest cheerleaders in life. We are truly blessed!

My dad's commitment to God is a priority. Mornings are for prayer and Bible reading, and Sundays are reserved for church. He knew that putting God first would set the foundation for everything else that came our way during the week. Even when work demanded his energy, he never compromised on faith. Church was a priority; it was a reminder that God always comes first, our lives belong to Him, and everything we have is a blessing from Him. He helped us cultivate an attitude of gratitude in our early years.

I never took for granted having my dad as a constant rock in our lives. While some of my friends grew up in fatherless homes, I always had my dad guiding, supporting, and loving me unconditionally, just like Jesus. I knew he was a man of his word who would follow through with his actions. He taught us the importance of reliability and responsibility early in life. He was present for many sporting events, concerts, challenges, and milestones such as my Quinceañera, graduations, baptism, the birth of my daughter, and my speaking engagements. I will never forget the days he coached our t-ball team. It meant so much that he would come home after working third shift or overtime many times exhausted, but he still made time for us.

When my own marriage ended after nearly ten years, my dad and mom took my daughter and me in without hesitation. He didn't just provide shelter, he gave us a home filled with love, faith, and security. During my darkest moments, his presence reminded me that I was never alone. I love how Jesus sends us these sweet reminders through our earthly fathers. Whether it was driving me to doctor's appointments or taking my daughter to her favorite places so I could work, he was always there for us. Every. Single. Time.

My dad didn't just offer help; he offered hope. He made sure I knew that setbacks didn't define me and that moving forward with God's help was possible, no matter how daunting it seemed. Con Dios todo es posible (With God, anything is possible). He isn't just a father; he is a living reminder of God's relentless support through every trial.

My dad finds pure joy in spending time with his grandkids. Whether he is cheering at games, telling jokes, watching movies together, dancing, traveling to the beach, eating at Freddy's or Orange Leaf, shopping at Five Below for toys, playing games at Peter Piper Pizza, making every moment fun. His lighthearted spirit creates lasting memories with them. All the grandkids absolutely adore their fun-loving Papa.

Dad's heart for service never runs dry. He'll drop whatever he's doing to help my brothers with car or house issues, run errands for me and my mom, or take my daughter to practices or classes. Whether inviting neighbors to church, helping family or friends with difficult tasks, or taking road trips to visit family in La Grulla, he gives of his time, treasure, and talents freely. He has even helped raise a few of his nephews, and he opens our home to any family member in need of a place to stay.

He knows that God has blessed him, and he believes it's his responsibility to bless others in return. His generosity has impacted more lives than he will ever know. It's truly inspiring! He is undoubtedly leaving a beautiful legacy of service that has helped shape how I love and serve others.

I will never forget how my dad stood by my side during the fight of my life battling a severe case of Lupus. During a college speaking engagement, I had my first unexpected seizure, and my dad tried to catch me as I collapsed. I can only imagine how helpless he must have felt, trying to save me from something completely beyond his control.

I spent 25 days in the hospital, flatlined three times, and some of those days unconscious. My loving parents were constantly by my bedside. My dad helped brush my teeth and hair, fed me, helped me walk, fulfilled my odd requests, and prayed over me. He navigated that dark time with prayer, gentleness, love, bravery, and compassion. He was my protector, my rock, and my constant comfort. I will always admire how he and my mom faced that nightmare with resilient faith and stepped up to help me through a long season of rehabilitation.

My dad's outgoing nature and humor light up every room, whether chatting at the grocery store, doctor's office, restaurant, or sharing jokes with neighbors and friends, he is a social butterfly that has never met a stranger. Now I know where we get it from!

I am proud to be his only daughter, forever a daddy's girl. His protective, supportive, and loving nature made growing up feel safe and cherished. I hope to find a husband one day who embodies my dad's greatest qualities.

I am blessed to carry on the Rodriguez/Solis legacy as a bestselling author, inspirational speaker, mentor, teacher, coach, founder of Sol2Soul and Shine Your Light Christian Camp and Youth Programs, and co-founder of Kingdom Youth Legacy. I'm grateful to raise my

13-year-old daughter, Hope, with the same values my dad instilled in me—faith, family, love, and hard work.

I know there are days you wonder if starting out as a poor little Mexican boy from both La Grulla, Texas and Hoopeston, Illinois with calloused hands and dusty boots really mattered, but I want you to know that God took your humble beginnings and wrote a mighty legacy with them.

Daddy, your hard working hands built a safe home for us. Your three children stand taller, dream bigger, and walk bolder. We are living proof that your labor was not in vain. We carry the legacy torch you lit with determination, purpose, and a fierce love for God and family.

You didn't just pave a path for us, you blazed a trail, ignited by Jesus and the footsteps of our grandfathers who began laying the way before you. You turned a small-town story into a generational blessing.

Your journey hasn't just impacted our family; it's touched everyone who knows you. You've faced challenges, made sacrifices, and worked tirelessly, not just to provide, but to inspire us to dream bigger and achieve more.

Daddy, you are a living example of God's provision and grace, teaching us that life's hardships can become blessings when faced with faith and perseverance (Romans 8:28). You remind me so much of your father-in-law, my grandpa Liborio "Louie" Rodriguez, one of your best friends. I miss him and my abuelo, Israel Solis Sr., dearly.

Thank you for being a father who leads with love, a husband who stays true, and a man who follows God's call. Your loyal commitment to faith and family is a gift I will never take for granted. Your scary quadruple bypass surgery was a wake-up call. God's given us borrowed time with you and we need to make every moment count.

I am forever grateful that God blessed us with the best Superman and Mr. Fix-It dad. You've shown us that love doesn't just endure, it thrives when rooted in faith and service. Your life is a living testament to God's faithfulness, reminding us to walk humbly with Him and to serve others with a grateful heart.

To everyone reading this: your hard work and sacrifices do not go unnoticed by God. Keep the faith, and continue building the legacy you want to leave behind. My dad's story shows that greatness isn't measured by where you start, but by how faithfully you walk the path God sets before you.

I wrote this chapter to honor you, dad, Ramon Solis Sr., and my two grandfathers, Liborio "Louie" Rodriguez and Israel Solis Sr., whose tireless work and steadfast faith paved the way for us to live the American dream. We are here today because of God's grace and the selfless sacrifices of the generations who came before us.

Daddy, you often joke, "Not too bad for a little Mexican from La Grulla," but the truth is, you are a gift from heaven. You are the rock we lean on, the roots that ground us, and the steady hand that's quietly guided us through every season of life.

I thank God every day for blessing us with you: a loving, devoted father, a faithful leader, and a man who embodies strength with tenderness. I couldn't think of a more meaningful way to celebrate you this Father's Day than by honoring your legacy in this book.

You've also done a good job modeling fatherhood for my brothers, Ramon Solis Jr. and Taylor Solis, who are not only great brothers but also amazing husbands and fathers to their families.

You have so many extraordinary accomplishments to look back on and smile about. I believe that at the end of your life, God will say, "Well done, my good and faithful servant."

Join me in continuing this legacy of faith, family, love, and purpose. Let's light up the world together—one word, one book, one speaking engagement, one camp, one retreat, and one youth program at a time.

You can connect with me at: <u>linktr.ee/EvelinaSolis</u>

JOIN THE MOVEMENT!
#BAUW

Becoming An Unstoppable Woman
With She Rises Studios

She Rises Studios was founded by Hanna Olivas and Adriana Luna Carlos, the mother-daughter duo, in mid-2020 as they saw a need to help empower women worldwide. They are the podcast hosts of the *She Rises Studios Podcast* and Amazon best-selling authors and motivational speakers who travel the world. Hanna and Adriana are the movement creators of #BAUW - Becoming An Unstoppable Woman: The movement has been created to universally impact women of all ages, at whatever stage of life, to overcome insecurities, and adversities, and develop an unstoppable mindset. She Rises Studios educates, celebrates, and empowers women globally.

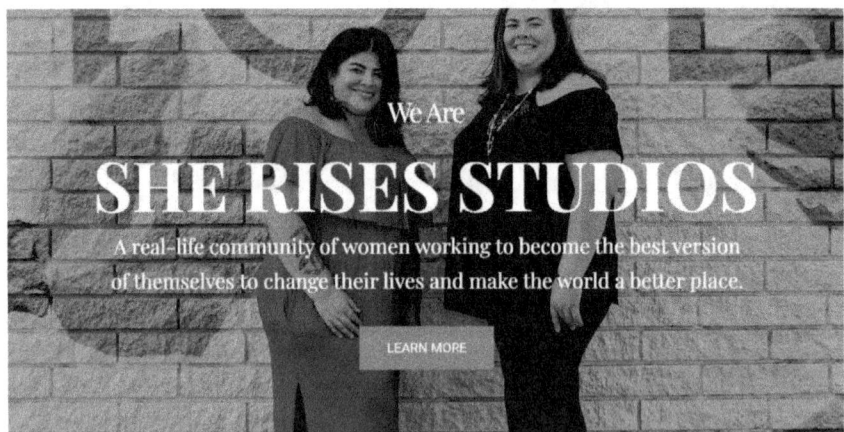

Looking to Join Us in our Next Anthology or Publish YOUR Own?

She Rises Studios Publishing offers full-service publishing, marketing, book tour, and campaign services. For more information, contact info@sherisesstudios.com

We are always looking for women who want to share their stories and expertise and feature their businesses on our podcasts, in our books, and in our magazines.

SEE WHAT WE DO

OUR PODCAST	OUR BOOKS	OUR SERVICES

Be featured in the Becoming An Unstoppable Woman magazine, published in 13 countries and sold in all major retailers. Get the visibility you need to LEVEL UP in your business!

Have your own TV show streamed across major platforms like Roku TV, Amazon Fire Stick, Apple TV and more!

Learn to leverage your expertise. Build your online presence and grow your audience with FENIX TV.
https://fenixtv.sherisesstudios.com/

Visit www.SheRisesStudios.com to see how YOU can join the #BAUW movement and help your community to achieve the UNSTOPPABLE mindset.

Have you checked out the *She Rises Studios Podcast?*

Find us on all MAJOR platforms: Spotify, IHeartRadio, Apple Podcasts, Google Podcasts, etc.

Looking to become a sponsor or build a partnership?

Email us at info@sherisesstudios.com